A Religion Called "Human"
A Case for "Positive" Secularism

Chanakya Ganguly

PublishAmerica
Baltimore

© 2005 by Chanakya Ganguly.
All rights reserved. No part of this book may be reproduced, stored in a retrieval system or transmitted in any form or by any means without the prior written permission of the publishers, except by a reviewer who may quote brief passages in a review to be printed in a newspaper, magazine or journal.

First printing

ISBN: 1-4137-8489-5
PUBLISHED BY PUBLISHAMERICA, LLLP
www.publishamerica.com
Baltimore

Printed in the United States of America

Wish you all the best in life

Regards!
Chandhu

A Religion Called "Human"
A Case for "Positive" Secularism

TABLE OF CONTENTS

Synopsis. 9
Dedication 13
Acknowledgments 17
Preface 19
Chapter 1: Assimilation 23
Ch 2: A Religion called Human. 26
Ch 3: Cultivation of Diversity. 34
Ch 4: Prisoner of Roots and Master's of Status Quo. 37
Ch 5: Living Life Through Work and Knowledge. 41
Ch 6. Creativity and Not Just Happiness to Live For. 45
Ch 7. Celebrating People, Life, and Technology. 48
Ch 8. Objective Art. 53
Ch 9. Love and Relationships. 56
Ch 10. Love and Marriage 59
Ch 11. Cultivating Emotional Balance 62
Ch 12. The Art of Communication 70
Ch 13. Fasting and Feasting. 73
Ch 14. Man is NOT a machine 76
Ch 15. Poverty of the Mind and Heart 80
Ch 16. Meditation and Compassion 83
Ch 17: On Pilgrimage 90
Ch 18: Beyond Nations & Religions—Global Citizen. 92
Ch 19: Conclusion of the Journey 95
Ch 20. The End 100
Ch 21: A Way Ahead—Be a Polymath 103
Ch 22: The Song of Silence 109
APPENDIX: Summary of Religion 111
Reference: Energy of Life. 113
Afterword. 117
Sequel: A Path of an Engineer 120
Epilogue. 125
Bibliography. 131

Synopsis

Religion should limit itself to human character and human values.

Human mind, spirit, and *creativity* are the *only* religions worth pursuing. The rest are all questionable. Instead of paying money for religious causes, one should find new ways of learning about art and creativity and paying creative people—like poets, artists, singers, theater artists, writers, library-builders, teachers, architects, doctors, researchers, scientists, engineers, sportsmen, and coaches. Eventually, by ignoring these people, we are going to kill our own real spiritual and creative self and be completely domesticated and controlled by rich people and nations, corrupt businessmen, fundamentalists, the madly religious, and the mentally weak, and we'll live the life of clerks and mobs.

Real creativity, spirituality, and religion are for the lion-hearted, not for the frightened and the chicken-hearted, who sit on the judgment of others. Hence, the religious nations rarely produce Olympic athletes, scientific innovations, engineering feats, medical wonders, planners, sensitive architects, designers, or builders of truly humanistic solutions.

"Freedom of expression" is one of the greatest spiritual qualities than every man possesses, and it needs to be appreciated and realized!!! The more a society allows such expressions to reverberate democratically, the less are its chances of stagnation, and the more are its chances of perpetual growth. I believe that life has to combine the secular and the sacred: both the gentle and the aggressive. Both can coexist harmoniously. Secularism, Humanism, and Universalism are the ways to go. As Raja Rammohun Roy, the founder of the Brahmo Samaj, said, "Testing, questing, and never resting, with open mind and open heart".

Whatever I have written in my book is the outcome of a very nice therapeutic process, which is basically called "freedom of expression". I think the process is very cathartic and healing. Many people misunderstand my style of communication. But, actually, this whole catharsis has had a very calming and creative effect on me. Whenever I am writing, I am actually writing or speaking, and I am actually very calm from inside. I genuinely feel that a man is neither arrogant nor humble; s/he just expresses his or her consciousness naturally: sometimes with aggression and passion, and sometimes with humbleness. I have found quite a bit of success in this therapeutic process of creativity, and it helps resolve conflicts within ourselves. It helps us in shedding all sorts of hypocrisy, lies, and dogmatism.

I think we should believe in the "force of argument" rather in the "argument of force"! If someone finds my writing repugnant, it should be refuted in writing. However, harsh words, as far as I'm concerned, are not conducive to spiritual well-being! The Desiderata says, "go placidly amidst the noise and haste, and remember what peace there may be in silence. Avoid loud persons; they are a vexation to the spirit". But I have learnt silence. The battle always starts from within. The first of it all being the conviction that what we know is not absolute, and, hence, is not the only way! That does not mean being stupid! In life, good intentions are not enough; it has to be communicated, acted, and persisted upon.

Dedication

This book draws deep inspiration from the writings of several visionaries who were Global Citizens, as well—the Buddha, Tagore, Dalai Lama, Krishnamurti, Gibran, Osho, Thomas Jefferson, John Milton, Thomas Paine, Ralph Waldo Emerson, Dom Moraes, architect Lawrie Baker, Octavio Paz, Henry David Thoreau, Rammohun Roy, Kant, Socrates, Lao-Tzu, Einstein, Larry Flynt, Jesus, Jawaharlal Nehru, actor Donald Sutherland, film directors Satyajit Ray, Gautam Ghosh, Mahesh Bhatt, and many other sensitive global citizens. This is dedicated to them.

I would also like to dedicate my book to many singers and their songs; learning and singing has also played a major role in my transformation. They are: Bhupen Hazarika (Songs: a. I am a Vagabond; b. Man is for Man, Life is for Life; c. Around the Vast Land on both sides, in the midst of millions of people, screaming in pain and anguish, O River Ganges, why do you flow so silently, without showing any concern?), John Lennon (Songs: Imagine: there's no countries and no religion too, nothing to kill or die for), Rod Stewart (Songs: Forever Young; Rhythm of my Heart, Beating like a Drum, words I love you rolling off my tongue…Where the ocean meets the sky I will be sailing), Nat King Cole (Songs: a. Unforgettable; b. Ramblin Rose; c. Mona Lisa), Frank Sinatra (Songs: a. I've Got the World on a String; b. My Way; c. Young at Heart; d. Come Fly With Me; Come Dance With Me), Billy Joel (Songs: Sing us a Song you're the Piano Man, sing us a song tonight, well, we're all in the mood for a melody, and you've got us feelin' alright), and the rustic Willie Nelson.

I have written this book after intense reflection and after having taken full responsibility for my life, and in the process, I have started changing it.

The book aims to rekindle the great spirit of "renaissance", which started in Europe and brought meaning and purpose to life and humanity. The essence of which was expressed by the great sculptor, Michelangelo, who at age 89 said, 'The end has come. But I just started understanding my profession.' Such was the depth and intensity, the passion and urge to be profusely creative and involved in one's work.

The root cause of "corruption" is "hypocrisy", i.e., lying to oneself. This exists when there is no harmony between the outer and inner, when one believes in falsehoods, when there is no conviction or inner fulfillment in one's thoughts, feelings, and actions, when there is no self-belief nor determination, and when a severe lack of appreciation of the beauty of the human mind, human spirit, and human creativity exists (and as a result of the struggle and effort to learn, realize, and recognize the same in an individual and every human being). This causes robotisation, exploitation, and decadence.

The human mind and human language are commensurate. So wherever there is any decline of correctness, precision, adequacy, and elegance in the use of a language, there is bound to be a matching decline in the power of the mind. The mind loses its depths, its intensity, and its capacity for making distinctions and accepts brutishness, incivility, and decadence.

Let's all sing a song, write a book, run a mile, build a house, or design a machine so that when death comes knocking at our door, we can say that we were very thankful to existence for letting us unravel the mysteries of life—and the seed has traveled far to become a flower.

Let's associate the human mind, body, and spirit with communication and creativity with every human being in all spheres of life—Science, Arts, Technology, Sports—focusing on real life issues like: poverty, disease, and death to make life really meaningful and respectful. This could be a way to humanize us all.

Acknowledgments

I would like to thank my uncle, D. Indu, my father, H.K. Ganguly, and my mother, Roma Ganguly, for having inspired me all of my life, although I did not agree with many of their ideas or suggestions. I rebelled always with a "positive" cause close to my heart. I also thank my music teacher, Elizabeth Hunter, from Atlanta, who inspired me with her music lessons on Western Classical, as well as for the plays we wrote and rehearsed together. I also thank Shaidu Kiven, my friend and room-mate from Cameroon, in Atlanta, for sharing much of his wisdom of the Bahais. I also thank Ashar Mahboob, my Pakistani room-mate in New Jersey, with whom I shared the pleasure of drinking and discussing. Many thanks to Daniel, my colleague in SITA, Singapore, who gave me Tai-Chi lessons and shared other Chinese wisdom. I also thank Fred Marie, my ex-colleague and boss in SITA, Atlanta who shared with me his vision of one-world, high technology and Akido. I also thank other SIAC/NYSE folks who inspired me like David Potochnack (now of DigitalArts) and Joanne Diehl (now of Think International). I also thank Sam Pitroda (now of WorldTel) and Shashi Tharoor (of United Nations) for their inspiring speeches in the Festival of India, in Atlanta, and for many of their writings.

I thank my sweet wife, Rangoli Sen and my other friends, Nagender Madavaram, Mukund Kher, and Arnab Dutta Roy for reviewing my writings. I also thank Aaron Desylva, L. Suresh Kumar, and Sudipta Sarkar for letting me break the fundamentalist mindsets, and thus, enlighten all of us. I am grateful to my friend, Dylan Lobo, who introduced me to the Habitat for Humanity, where I had a great experience of building houses in Atlanta, and in the process listened to Rosalyn Carter speak about her efforts on the protection, preservation, diagnosis, and cure for mental health. I am thankful to M.N.Rao, Sunder Rajan, and Subhadra Vemuri, who introduced me to technology, literature, and hiking during my first job with TCS, in Bombay, where we had fun trekking the Sahydris and dreaming globally. I am thankful to Ayush Agrawal and Valinder Mangat for having inculcated in me a spirit of entrepreneurship and who also went sailing with me in the Arabian Sea in a spirit of fun, freedom, playfullness, and adventure. I thank Vishy Dasari of ObjectNet Technologies for listening and for commenting on my ideas and experiments on spirituality, religion, and technology. I also want to thank Subhankar Choudhury for giving me the impetus to go ahead with my book by converting the first plain text notepad document to a nice MS Word format.

Preface

Mind creates science; the heart creates religion. Mind can give better science and better technology. The heart gives the inner values: love, truth, freedom, and awareness. We can't digest this simple thing and divide ourselves into secular, communal, Hindu, Muslim, Jewish, Christian, theist, atheist, god, goddess, caste, or sub-caste; the list goes on and on. We must just accept that we are "human". Hence, Bahaullah said, "life has to combine science with religion". Life is about the joy of engaging and growing ourselves from many directions by constant mutation, addition, substraction, re-interpretation, re-invention, self-discovery, and thus the constant flow of energy.

Freedom is important, but does it mean a free for all. It should be about our ability to connect our thoughts, Feelings and actions with our abilities, experience, state of knowledge, motive, and its impact on us, people, life, and the environment. Hence, we have manufactured new, violent social values.

In general, people are reluctant to change and hence like to cling to a virtual concept called religion where they find solace in having connection with the so-called constant entity. Just by making the development of our own self through our—body, mind, emotions, intellect, creativity, and consciousness—through various situations, experiences, education, innovation, motivation and learning in life, we can make that the constant. Nobody is a follower, nobody is a leader; we then become fellow travelers sharing love, understanding, knowledge, wisdom and clarity. We are all part of the Earth Democracy which we can rebuild today.

Organized religions are like a deep cauldron. There is some truth, but there are many things which are irrelevant to a certain time and space. The important part is to be able to reinvent oneself again and again and move things to museums. Some are claiming that they know the last real words of God. Some are involved in worshipping images, believing in clerics, priests, gurus, superstitions, rituals, astrologers, pilgrimages, and holy dips. All are involved in humiliating themselves. Some are involved in torturing women in the name of some archaic redundant laws. Some have taken refuge in the past in the name of karma and transmigration of the souls; some have taken refuge in the future, beyond death. But all that is happening is happening in life, right in front of us, and they are all postponing it. Religion is one. As Frank Sinatra said, he feels that the music that goes closest to the heartbeat is the most natural and rhythmic tempo and so has been the history of music. Hence, in life, we also need to find that rhythm for our own harmony.

Chapter 1: Assimilation

Assimilation of global values—the best that the world can provide—can well be achieved through the various shades of friendship that we build around ourselves. This cuts across all kinds of prejudged notions and values systems from which we imprison ourselves, taking us back in time.

"Friendships" can happen at all kinds of intellectual, spiritual, and emotional levels; it does not always have to be a physically intimate or an emotionally charged one, which I think should exist only in long-term, committed relationships. At a rational level, intellectual and spiritual friendships can open our minds and hearts to new ideas and opportunities; ever seeking, ever building, ever creating.

A friendship could be made with a singer singing on the streets, or with a tourist from a distant nation going on a river cruise, or with a nice professional who is working on his/her computer keyboard. They are all trying to make sense of what life is all about: pursuing one's dreams, goals, and just living life. It is more important to celebrate this human spirit in the common man trying to do extraordinary, or even ordinary things, rather than talk about God, Destiny, Sin, Salvation, or other virtual things.

It does not really matter if God exists or does not exist, but what definitely matters is human character and human values. Life is a journey that allows us to go through diverse experiences in building and developing our *body, mind, emotions, intellect, creativity and consciousness, and a sense of concern* for a fellow-human and other living beings and the environment as rationally as possible. This journey, I think, is what should be celebrated through assimilation of diverse values and knowledge.

As the great Indian thinker, economist and politician, Chanakya (Kautilya) said, "There is some self-interest behind every friendship. There is no friendship without self-interests. This is a bitter truth". Hence, let us be very frank and free about keeping our friendships with people in the context with which we relate best to them, and which helps each of us grow continuously in the five directions mentioned above. To grow as individuals, to display our skills, to learn and unlearn continuously, we need the collective. Extreme individualism can make us neurotic, and extreme collectivity can make us a police state. Hence, there is the middle path of moderation and balance. Let us fulfill our desires rationally without causing destruction. Chanakya also said, "A person should not be too honest. Straight trees are cut first, and honest people are screwed first". Hence, this is a good lesson in self-preservation and safety consciousness. He also said, "Jealousy is another name for failure". And to add further, "Once you start working on something, don't be afraid of failure, and don't abandon it. People who work sincerely are the happiest."

Chapter 2: A Religion Called *Human*

Dare to know; dare to use your own intelligence. Thus beseeched the German philosopher Immanuel Kant against organized authority of religion. Religion in ancient times came as a packaged deal of ethics, mind control, management, professions, as well as some music and prayers to keep the minds of people engaged so that they would not harm others.

But in modern times, as science and technology have improved, people are mixing with each other all over the world. There are many engaging hobbies and activities to keep oneself involved; there is no need for such a religion anymore. Religion need only be confined to the extent of human characters and human values, which basically boils down to freedom with responsibility and concern for fellow human-beings, (and every other living organism and the environment around us as rationally as possible) without creating a mess around. There are only two people who we know as of this date who never claimed that they were messengers of god. One is the Buddha, and the other is Mahavira. They only promoted the use of one's own intelligence, as well as fearlessness, compassion, and courage.

We need not think that those messengers or books contain more intelligence than what we already have. Probably if the same messengers came today, they would have given some other message, since religion always comes into our minds.

It is basically a very boring activity. Many concepts of castes were kept earlier in Hinduism, as there was no proper education system to train people. Hence, the caste system was a way to propagate professions and sustain society. But there is no meaning of such things in the modern context. It has crippled society with its own feudalistic chains and has served to tie us down.

An universal caste called "human" should be declared and accepted by the masses, instead of playing politics and using "reservations". Instead, every idea should be debated and discussed by scientists, professionals, psychologists, and psychiatrists in a democratic set-up.

Almost all the Western countries became secular inspite of having only one religion called Christianity because religion is basically common sense and human values; beyond that it should promote physical and mental strength and rational independent thinking and creativity. Thus secularism, humanism, and universalism can only benefit people.

As Salman Akhtar, professor of psychiatry at Jefferson Medical College, Philadelphia and lecturer at Harvard Medical School, writes, "We start as parental fantasies and die as our grandchildren's memories. Reality is always a hybrid. Purity is an attack on reality turning complexity with simplicity. Prayer or religion, theism or atheism is fine, as long as it does not promote grandiose thoughts, and as long as it seeks to instill peace, kindness, humility, and tolerance. Fundamentalism leads to megalomania and violence. It benefits nobody."

In our life, we have a very small energy. Instead of wasting our time in such futile talks, we need to keep our focus in the development of the *body, mind, emotions, intellect, creativity, and consciousness* with a sense of concern for fellow human-beings (and every other living being and the environment as rationally as possible). All we need is to develop resources and train people so there is an interdependent economy of people with various skills and techniques so that each individual develops these five characteristics within himself/herself.

This enlightenment already came in Christianity with the renaissance that happened in Europe. That is why in the Western world, every ordinary person silently focuses on developing oneself in these areas, and nobody is really looked down upon by the money that one earns or does not earn. But in religion-oriented countries, we look for extraordinary people to take us through and solve all of our problems in life, instead of democratically debating, discussing, and doing it ourselves. Hence, instead of looking inwards, we look outwards and thus fall victim to power-hungry politicians and engage in argumentative discussions.

Most countries have enough brains, resources, and skills to develop a vibrant economy to support itself, especially if we look for solutions outside the realm of religion and focus on the real development of the person.

Our evolution with the resources available should be our purpose in Life. And as we grow in wisdom we can pass on our knowledge, wisdom, education, creativity to create more resources and strive to balance between the individual and the collective as one does not have any meaning without the other. This would help fight wars, poverty and violence. And thus we promote progress and sustainable development.

We try to ape the West and then instead of developing ourselves—creatively by say learning music, or composing a song, or writing book, or playing hockey, or learning new science, technology, software, hardware concepts and engaging ourselves in creativity we try to buy big houses, expensive cars, and then go to priests and temples. Religion is for the creative and lion-hearted who do not sit on the judgement of others.

To me spirituality, means the various ways we can connect with each other and the environment and various forces around us—knowledge, education, wisdom, economics, political, social, and yet be able to introspect and keep our calmness and integrity and yet be aggressive enough to harmonize our inner yearnings with these forces and resources with a constructive motive.

Real spirituality is basically "right concentration" to whatever we do, or whatever problem one is trying to solve. One must do it very intelligently in order to increase one's endurance and creativity to higher levels. It could be playing hockey with full concentration, or running a mile, or writing a book, or designing complex software.

It is like buying a pair of Reebok shoes but never running a mile. It's like buying an expensive music system, but having no clue about music, or basically the fun in exercising ourselves or going to a teacher and learning to sing, or landscaping an area or building a house. It's like having a swimming pool, but sipping whiskey and having kebabs around the pool and then going for meditations and art of living classes.

All we have to remember is that life is an operating system, and one has to use one's time, money, energy, and resources so that based on the current economic scenario of the country, one can meaningfully develop oneself from all the 5 sides—body, mind, emotions, intellect, creativity, and consciousness. Creativity is not restricted to the arts only. It is basically doing one's profession well, one's hobbies well, developing diverse skills which interest oneself, and eating the right food.

All that we need to do is to develop our physical, mental and emotional strength so that we can handle the ups and downs of life, as well as other diverse situations, and, hence, enable us to be able to handle various situations fearlessly. That will develop faith in our own self, and we can also have faith in God, as that is basically the highest form of abstraction. This enables us to know that we are part of the ecosystem of the planet, and, thus, part of the Universal Intelligence.

We need to solve life's problems with education, knowledge, science and rationality. As Thomas Jefferson said, "even if there was a God, he will be open to reason."

This will only benefit us in making our minds stronger and in making our own destiny through learning. Life will always have the problem of ego, grief, death, and disease.

We may not be directly working in our fields of learning but since everything impacts everything else, we may intelligently find ways of using one skill and implementing it in some other field. Like learning to sing or do theatre can help develop our communication, leadership, and presentation skills in our job in a more fun, deep, and creative way. Learning sports helps us develop our endurance and gives us a respect for our body, which develops our health, energy, endurance, lifestyle, and our overall immune system. Team sports also help us to strategize and use our mind and energy effectively. We learn time-management and energy-utilization. Understanding medicine, herbs, and massage helps us understand the body, its organs, nutrition, the prevention and correction of diseases and how it impacts healthcare, economics, and insurance. We may also learn about communicable diseases and its relation to waste disposal, pollution, or environmental damage and how we can correct the same.

Thus there may be other fields like environmental engineering or automotive design or municipal design or pollution control or hazardous wastes or healthcare or actuary or quality control and we would then understand how various professions are in many ways interdependent of each other and also to similar problems of human health, innovation, and managing civic amenities. We may be in legal professions or finance or accounting or taxation and we will be able to visualize the motive behind compliance or regulations for restaurants or building design or safety measures or highway speed design or traffic engineering and also its relation to physics, friction, chemistry, civil engineering, material science, and the various gadgets and equipments developed for simulation, modeling, automation and design using electronics, computers, hydraulics, robotics etc.

The more we do live life consciously every moment becomes an opportunity for growth. We value our abilities and seek to develop more in the context of living life, working, expressing ourselves effectively as well as efficiently, thus learning to communicate at the right level in the right context to the right person to fulfill each other's needs without creating too much heat, damage, and destruction. We value the assets and materials whether it is a home or a car or a music system or television or computers and learn to protect it and make the most effective utilization of these for our growth. Luck is the meeting of realistic aspirations with opportunities going past us all the time.

That is why Guru Nanak called his religion Sikhism. That means "be a life long student". To learn is to become religious. This can be practiced at home, at the office, at the marketplace, at play —in every moment of life. There is no need to go to the temple, mosque, church, or gurdwara. The word disciple is beautiful; it means "one who is capable of learning". It comes from a root word which means 'learning'. One who is capable of learning is a disciple.

Osho says in the book *Tantric Transformations,* "Become disciples of your own life. Life is really our master. And if one cannot learn from life, where else can one learn from? If even the great master life is defeated by you and cannot teach you anything, then who will be able to teach you anything?"

We do not want to be prejudiced or polarize ourselves with unreal things. There is enough in reality that would exhaust hundreds of lifetimes. We would like to see both sides of everything and focus on the positive side to bring about change, learning, and improvement. Then there is nothing wrong. We always find solutions to problems based on the state of our knowledge. We maintain the bottomline of how we are interconnected in this time and space through our body, mind, emotions, intellect, and creativity and thus try to expand our life and consciousness from many dimensions. Be it doing cooking, cleaning, interior design, form, function, time, space, architecture, resource economics, public vs. private space, learning music—vocal or instrumental, theater or writing, science, technology, medicine, electronics, and so on.

They build their own temples within themselves; they fight their own jihad within themselves; they start their own conversions within themselves. They do not build temples elsewhere; they do not fight jihad elsewhere; and they do not convert other people. They fight to become Universal Humans.

Chapter 3: Cultivation of Diversity

Monocultures breed insanity and polarize societies. They promote militancy and fanaticism. To live life in today's world, one needs to constantly expand one's horizons and practice conscious and constant cultivation of diversity.

As biodiversity is needed for the survival, growth, and mutation of stronger, healthier and more creative species in nature, so is it needed in societies.

It is interesting to go to depths of diversity and find the basic, unifying commonality amongst all. Diversity stimulates creativity and allows millions of possibilities to happen, and, thus, does not keep the society static.

Stagnation in life, culture, knowledge, and society leads to degeneration. Only a highly flexible and elastic mind, backed up by good values and decision making abilities, can keep thriving in this world. One should not feel guilty about the decisions that one takes in life, but one should rather learn to cope with them. The greatest challenge in life is to make choices amongst the infinite alternatives and possibilities that life presents to us. Thus, decision making should not be based on emotions, but rather on good values and a bright future. It should stimulate a vision in a person which arouses a sense of conviction in him or her, and which can be backed up by planned and creative actions. A life without vision may as well run into a hallucination and depression.

We need to constantly interpret, reinterpret, add, subtract, learn, unlearn, and relearn the various actions we undertake in our lives. Diversity allows us to constantly reevaluate ourselves and makes us free from dogmatism or the feeling that we are always right, or our way is the perfect way, and the rest is the highway. The conflict in our mind and psyche later escalates into the physical and sometimes manifests into physical and psychological violence. We need to pursue clarity of thought and purpose all the time. We need to learn the importance of creativity, communication, debating, discussing, dialogue, exchange, flow, growth, and free-thinking.

We should not get stuck with some structure or utopia or some bookish knowledge only. In real life, we need to "reform" the box, which suits the requirements of the situation. Our solutions should be more participatory and inclusive in nature. We need to foster entrepreneurial thinking rather than managerial thinking. As long as we can align all our positive and negative forces with a zeal to live and explore work and life, a positive discontent also helps. Grey hairs have their own beauty in life. There are no fixed rules in dealing with situations. We can make changes and revolutions, but that could be a move from the frying pan to the fire if we do not take into account the prevailing culture and situation. A good entrepreneur creates a different path by getting into the culture of a system. Otherwise, one may easily get frustrated and throw up arms. There is something we learn from instinct and experience. We need to learn not only to manage the egos of others, but to subdue our own, as well. Many people have bloated egos based on virtual and superficial ideas. It is high time that we "rebel" to unite.

Chapter 4: Prisoner of Roots and Masters of the Status Quo

"Roots" has been a well-acclaimed word going around the world for quite sometime. But with today's mobile and diverse population interacting with each other all over the world, the possibility of growing one's own roots in a foreign soil and assimilating new roots within oneself has become a definite need and possibility. Today, one need not be a prisoner of one's roots anymore. With the internet, telecommunication, television, radio, and jet travel all around the world, the possibility of breaking away from one's roots, if it is not producing the desired results anymore, and creating a set of new roots for oneself has become a positive choice to go for.

We are all born in some family, receive some kind of education, grow up in a certain political climate, with certain economic conditions and religion. Most of us get totally conditioned by these factors and never try to think critically to break out of all barriers and conditioning to make choices not based on inheritance or conditioning, but based on the fact that we dare to know, dare to use our own intelligence. Then all these pathologies and obsessions about pride and honor, money, culture, religion and family disappear. A person becomes creative and starts discovering his or her unique and true self. He listens to his heart—his intuitions backed up by ever expanding experience, knowledge, wisdom on various aspects and dimensions about life, growth, and the world in general.

There is no meaning in saying that one belongs to this religion or that faith. Religion is one and that is development of knowledge and its application in life through actions. It needs maturity, wisdom, and understanding about existence, coexistence, and reality.

Books, traditions, and rituals are passed on, hence we have to use reason and use our time and energy fruitfully. The significant thing to remember is one has to re-evaluate, re-invent, and keep what makes sense and reject the rest.

Tagore wrote a poem titled, "Dhula Mandir" (meaning "Temple of Dust"). He found God in the sweat of the farmers and the workers and not in the incense sticks, mantras and beads. It is a waste of time going to the temples, churches and mosques (read museums), visiting the gurus, priests, clerics, and astrologers (read magicians), or reading holy books (read spiritual fiction) that talk about some "virtual world". Organized religions have all destroyed the human intelligence and killed too much in every man. They have all suffered from political corruption of religion.

A so-called religious or spiritual person is one who talks about holy books but has no real experience or understanding of life. S/he does not have the wisdom that comes by doing things using one's own mind and one's own hands. S/he just keeping repeating mantras and rituals, which is a very degrading activity. Believers are always blind. No wonder the so-called religious countries rarely produce athletes, scientists, innovators, medical wonders and have a hard time being democratic and debating on ideas, concepts, and ways of implementation. They are so contented in churning out mediocrity by the thousands and have no understanding of really what benefits their own very self.

What we really need is to follow our true potential to expand and excel. We can choose to remain mediocre and be slaves of politics, economics, religion, false ego, lies and negativity. But at the end, we are only answerable to our own self and stray away from realizing our destiny. Only the intensely focused enjoy this great existence.

Osho says in his book, *The Little Book of Osho*, "One has to be selfish, travel the path first, know perfectly well where it leads—only then can one hold hands of others. Only then can one be altruistic. First one should be rooted in one's own being, and then one will be able to help others".

When we are selfish initially, we are driven by our ego and energy to pursue growth, untill we grow in strength, confidence and creativity and come to the point of integration, where it can be thrown away. But one good principle to follow in life is to always be in the mode of teacher as well as student. One can even learn about new things from one's enemies. So it is said that it is better to have a clever enemy than a foolish friend. Life is like a river, and it should keep growing and flowing. Complacency makes us dead.

Life is a struggle, but with knowledge and confidence, that struggle becomes enjoyable and creative. The chaos slowly reduces to order. The chattering of the mind dwindles down to calmness of the rock. The competition and the concert becomes one and is harmonious. The two paradoxes dissolve, and we start to function easily with universal consciousness, and we discover new things with our intuition and experience.

We start to realize that all the problems and solutions start with our understanding of things in the right context in our mind, and we start to understand human behavior from what goes on in the mind. The more we keep ourselves grounded toward keeping a positive discontent for growth in life, and by not getting distracted by little successes, we keep running the marathon of life like Jesus or Socrates who said, "Be poor in spirit". That is existence. That is continuity. That is sustainability. We do not create a mess and leave this earth.

Chapter 5: Living Life Through Work and Knowledge

Living life through the right combination of work and knowledge lets one translate theory into practice, burn one's own hands, and does not allow one to remain an armchair intellectual who remains bookish without developing the wisdom and clarity that comes from doing things. This helps in innovation, connecting to real-life problems and situations from real experience and connecting with people and understanding their struggles and creativity and helping many who sometimes do not have the education or the power of the mind to automate menial jobs and thus improve productivity and quality. The whole practice keeps the body and mind as an integral whole.

One of the simplest and finest teachings of Hinduism is to lead the life of a King and a Sage at the same time—it is called "rajarshi". The West also calls such people

"Philosopher-Kings". The combination of these two attributes brings out the best qualities in a person, which are perennial and everlasting.

Ancient cultures need to resolve their crisis with modernity by relegating irrationality and reinventing some of their art, architecture, music, food, literature. Some of their medicinal systems could be researched using modern tools, science, technology to find anything worth preserving. That gives them self-esteem, pride, and a good self-concept and helps them accept modernity to create, invent, design, and accept modernity as a way to improve their quality of life. Since modernity arrived in most countries through colonization, hence, modernity is always looked upon as a suspect for cultural and economic imperialism because of an unbridging of the past and the present, and, hence, is looked upon as a tool of domestication and control rather than liberation. This results in poor leadership skills, poor self-concept, and a lack of creativity and innovation to design and evolve the system with the psyche of the nation. It causes violence, as the system is mostly put into place through an iron grip. Most people tend to think changing the Outer changes the inner. But the reality is only changing the inner changes the outer, not the other way. Hence, to resolve the conflicts and crisis with modernity, the inner psychology of the past needs to be bridged with the outer aspects of modernity for true development.

One of the crises we have with modernity is that one group of people is stuck to the past and cannot identify itself with modern reality, which makes many go into a contemplative mood, disconnecting from real world issues and many times getting mired into negativity.

And we have another group of people who are totally involved and corrupted by world affairs, who are enslaved by wealth, fame, status, money, and who get cozy management jobs, but have no in-depth technical know-how, whom Jack Welch of GE calls, "Kissing Up and Kicking Down".

What we need is a critical mass of people who will have the courage to combine the best of both worlds by being detached professionals who are grounded and who will continuously strive to evolve through work, knowledge, experience, and creativity and who will also possess people skills and leadership skills. This combination will be like the king and the sage, or the "Philosopher-King".

For them, poverty is about pockets. They do not understand that it is about an *uncreative* and *unproductive mind*. It is the *poverty of the mind and heart* that is the problem. The person who has realized this and works towards elimination of these can make the right use of money. Otherwise, the *richness of pockets* has no meaning. The poverty, the mediocrity, the confusion and lack of clarity and purpose goes on. Only changing the inner changes the outer, not the other way.

Osho says, "Man lives such a dull and drab life that they want some sensation. Those who are a little wise, they read scientific fiction. Those who are not so wise, they read spiritual fiction".

To it, we can add that we watch those violent movies and TV serials whose only storyline is revenge, emotional blackmail, and misunderstanding. The day we understand our insecurities and feel foolish about various rituals and fears—just sitting silently will be more than enough. The important thing in life is to be occupied with oneself—sometimes working individually and sometimes collectively—like playing violin or piano or singing a song in a concert making harmony.

Chapter 6: Creativity and Not Just Happiness to Live For

Happiness and pleasure have many times been espoused as the goals of living life. But it does not essentially give the essence of living and finding the meaning of life. The urge to create, the urge to grow, the strength to go through the burning fires of heaven and hell, happiness and misery, and yet come out with something creative at the end like the Agony and Ecstasy of Michelangelo, or the Lust for Life of Vincent Van Gogh, or other inventions and discoveries, the enterprise and creativity of so many scientists, engineers, doctors, musicians, painters, architects, sportsmen, and entrepreneurs is what should be celebrated and lived for. That urge to grow from deep within, which crosses all boundaries of fear and insecurity, and the conviction that arises out of a vision to pursue the same diligently and to keep creating, is something that needs appreciation.

The whole of the European Renaissance was filled with people who believed that work does not happen, but is what happens within oneself when doing work. That is the decisive one. If it brings light into one's being, if it brings a deep fulfillment, if it makes one more loving and more joyous, then it is absolutely relevant to what one is doing. Do it, and do it totally because the more totally one does it, the more intelligence one brings in doing it, and the more individuality then becomes authentic. The more one's potentiality become assured, the more one comes closer to one's destiny and to one's home. To find one's purpose is impossible without finding oneself, and the moment one finds oneself, simultaneously, one will find one's purpose. That is what made Michelangelo say, at the age of 89, that he had just started learning his profession. That is what the Buddha said is Right Concentration. He was a practical, earthy man. Buddha's approach is very pragmatic and scientific: What are the causes of suffering, and how can they be ended?

At 29, Buddha dropped the royal life of security, luxury, and pleasure, to which most people are naturally inclined, and began his wandering search for inner fulfillment. He shared his experiences and wisdom and never claimed to be a messenger of God. He propagated the idea of complete self-responsibility for one's thoughts, feelings and actions and devised the Eight Fold Path to Enlightenment: Right Understanding, Right Thoughts, Right Speech, Right Conduct, Right Livelihood, Right Effort, Right Mindfulness, and finally, Right Concentration, which would slowly but certainly lead to developing complete faith in one's own self.

Today, with modern science and technology, one can probably live longer and work more diligently, sincerely, and effectively and enjoy the same to the fullest. One can be an entrepreneur at a later stage in life, when one becomes more matured, understanding and confident, and once one develops a vision and approaches the same with flexibility, clarity, patience, and experimentation with a focused and organized mind and dedication. One can pursue various professions at various times in life as one's interests changes and evolves and as one wants to explore the many dimensions of life and our very earthly existence.

Chapter 7: Celebrating People, Life, and Technology

Many times we see life as only material growth. But we forget to see it as a whole. Growth should be in many directions: intellectual, social, psychological, physical, artistic, literary, and material, as well. We would probably not be so obsessed with money if we knew what we wanted to do with it. If only we just celebrated people, life, and technology all around us. A pro-life approach would allow us to compete and yet work in concert. The word "money" in Sanskrit is beautiful; it is called "Artha". And "Artha" has two definitions—money, as well as "meaning". So money, in many ways, is needed to find meaning in life. It is like a current, but one needs to know how to use it. So it is also called currency. Technology has been one of the greatest gifts of modern man. It has brought the world together and has accomplished what religion, economics, and many other things could not. It has allowed people to communicate, exchange, and rediscover each other and share their pains, aspirations, and goals. Technology, with a bit of an ethical imagination, is probably the greatest invention of man.

Muhammad said, "Every child is born a Muslim". That was the essence of his whole teaching. Religion needs the eyes of wonder of a child and a heart that can feel the awe of things around us. A truly religious person should be able to create, lead, or innovate and remove the poverty of the mind and the heart.

We need to act in harmony with our fellow beings, with nature, and with inanimate objects. We need to learn to let go of that which cannot be owned, or which is destroyed by grasping. We need to know that a thing or an action which may seem of little value to us, may be a priceless treasure to another. We need to know that there is no shame in questioning. We need to be diligent in our work and practice. We need to know that even great worldly wealth, and the accumulation of material things, are of little worth compared with the priceless treasures of love, peace, and the freedom to grow.

One needs to be aggressive in one's profession, and being positively belligerent is not bad. We need to don many hats in our live and learn from a variety of situations, professions, and experiences, and we must be be innovative and interdisciplinary. We can learn from sports, ethics, analysts, designers, detached professionals, and as well as from good managers and orators. We need to take some calculated risks and bold moves. We need to pursue life-long education, discipline, and rigorous analysis. We need controlled aggression. Aggression should be a motivation to excel. It should translate to an intense desire to solving problems. That needs energy and an effective use of resources and assertiveness. We need to be able to strategize and plan toward a vision with a mission and not fight with each other. We need to compete positively. Human beings are the same universally. We need to connect with people, have an understanding of the big picture, and yet have attention to detail rather than just use statistics. We need to learn from mistakes and not repeat them. We need to have facts with logical conclusions and not distort the same as politicians do.

Rob Thomas thumping in his "Something to Be" sings: "All the people in the world have come together, more than ever. I can feel it. We will make it through this somehow. I can feel it. Can you feel it? Telling you to hold tight. Things will be alright. Trying to find a better life. Let's your self go."

On the very long road, we need to create colleges and universities for interdisciplinary education, studies, research, and ideas that combine branches of engineering, arts, history, economics, management, politics, architecture, and environment with an underlying, ever-evolving philosophical framework in order to build a University of the Future to help make religion meaningful.

We need to combine technology, innovation, economics, and public policy in areas like urban planning, and with socio-economic indicators, surveillance systems, and forecasting systems. We need to combine computing with humanity and study human-computer interactions and graphics-visualization-usability for empowerment. We need to handle the situations of handicaps and disasters.

Today, nanotechnology sensory devices, transducers, and GPS systems, when combined with GIS and GSM systems for mobile telephony, can provide various navigational and management aids. Bio-medical devices can be produced in collaboration with chemical, mechanical, electronics, computer science, biology, and insights in medicine. Terabytes of data could be stored, retrieved, archived, and transmitted over high speed networks like ATM for MRI images and chem-informatics with molecular modeling for drug discovery, and so on.

Architecture, civil design, automotive CAD, and chip design can all be simulated and designed for robustness and disaster safety by combining graphics, simulation, modeling, engineering, art, science, human psychology, behavior, and cognition to give a new impetus to creativity, innovation, and consciousness. The computer has become a glue, and, hence, we can manage interdependent and yet independent systems like roads, water, phones, and power.

It could be things like the development of earthquake-proof housing, or the study of light-weight, durable materials, or the research on ecological housing, or water conservation that might optimize the use of time and space, form and function, as well as sustainable housing, such as in Japanese architecture. This involves interdisciplinary studies of material science, physics, civil engineering, and even computers for simulation.

The combination of economic incentives and the feedback system between academia, research, and the industry is needed for the evolution of mature systems going through constant change alongside the needs of the people, market, resources, energy, environment, and within the state of knowledge. Many a times, such interdisciplinary efforts lead to some other totally different innovation, which could be astroturf for sports like hockey, for example.

Chapter 8: Objective Art

In the book *Tantric Transformations*, Osho says, "In temples like Khajuraho, where all sorts of sexual postures are sculptured. These are examples of objective art. These temples were not pornographic, they were spiritual—transforming human energy towards higher levels. The energy has to be freed from the lower level. And to free it, there is only one way: to make it absolutely conscious, to bring all the fantasies of the unconscious mind to the conscious. When the unconscious is completely unburdened, one is free. Then one doesn't have any blocks, and then one can move inwards".

The key point to understand is when we are miserable or frustrated it is usually because we have an energy block. Hence, the cause of the blockage has to be identified and needs to be cleared by best diverting the energy to meaningful purposes that leads to growth.

Abstinence is the simple rationality of protecting ourselves from diseases. Promiscuity is the lack of love and respect for one's own body and another person's as it leads to abuse of the body, spread of diseases and unwanted pregnancies. Every human body should be respected as a work of art or sculpture.

The key point to understand is that everything has two sides. Pornography, strip clubs and good sex education about the human psychology and anatomy can liberate the mind from violence and perversions. As Larry Flynt quoted Milton saying it is no use complaining about the food but rather check our stomach when we become sick. It is the mind that needs to be evolved and fixed.

The image of Kali wearing a garland of human heads indicates the destruction of the human ego very beautifully, and her stepping on a lying Shiva indicates her sense of shame for stepping on ultimate freedom from spiritual slavery. Durga and her family indicate the need of freedom (Shiva), strength (Durga), wisdom (Ganesha), learning (Saraswati), wealth (Lakshmi), and adventurism (Kartikeya) as necessary to lead a balanced and successful life. These images are visual representations of human conditions and have an educational value for the masses.

Misery nourishes the ego. Transform your miseries to experiences of growth. One needs to experience good/bad, dark/light, and all the opposites to gain maturity. Money is important in modern life. But it is equally (if not more) important to understand that people control others by giving money and by not giving money, as well.

The huge amount of money, time, and energy that is spent in talking about religion, wars, nationalism, patriotism, weapons, freedom, faith, self-determination, and democracy can be invested in communications, sports, creativity, understanding, human development, art, music, science, health, technology, literature, building design, and research and development.

The ego can be crushed by: breaking free from the "I" and expanding into the universal consciousness; understanding various human conditions; and striving to achieve the big, expansive, "universal human" mind.

Chapter 9: Love and Relationship

Osho had said many times that the solution to eradicate prostitution is to remove the very concept of marriage. He feels that marriage leads to the concept of nation. Further, he notes that all marriages are a constant war zone which gets scaled to national levels and can be transmitted to children, as well. Plato also stressed the fact that marriages work negatively in curbing creative potential. But I do not fully agree with both of them.

Prostitution, in my opinion, is not just restricted to the commercial sex activity, which I think is very degrading and demeaning to humanity and should be banished from the face of the earth. But, to me, prostitution is about the inner psychology or physical activity without a deeper mental/spiritual/emotional connection and commitment between people.

To me, the solution for the HIV/AIDs menace is not just about condoms or abstinence, but is about debating and educating people about this inner psychology, and, hence, learning to appreciate and inculcate the art of nurturing and developing self-control, where one learns full self-responsibility in order to be able to handle his/her freedom meticulously and with a deep sense of concern.

A relationship works out well between two people when the communication is clear and the relation is founded upon some clearly communicated agenda or reality or common interest with the kind of stimulation, interests, plans, and duration in mind that binds the two people. This allows one to understand one's limits, boundaries, expectations and the positives and negatives in a relationship. Simplicity allows the achievement of a lot of complex issues very easily in a relationship. Thus, each is open about their strengths and weaknesses, the common interests of life that are complementary as well as supplementary. Hidden agendas always bring bad blood and bitterness, leading to manipulative tendencies and the urge to control.

A relationship flourishes, sustains, and grows when both parties keep watering their seeds of interest and keep learning, sharing, and promoting growth and creativity among each other whether in their common interests or enlightened self interest or in wisdom that develops in the process of tackling various problems, mysteries, and issues that each person faces in life and in seeking solutions and thus achieving a sense of pride and satisfaction.

In the process of seeking solutions through communication, learning, experience, capability, maturity, confidence and creativity, one becomes positively daring, strong, and free. One can then tap into various resources, people, knowledge, and potentials and bring out the beauty and energy of each other. And in the case of confusion, one can always fall back on the basic reference of growth and what one does and gains.

As Tuka says, "Don't crush a flower to possess its fragrance. Don't eat a baby because you love it. Don't try to lick the liquid glow of a pearl. Don't break a musical instrument to find out its sound. Don't covet the reward for doing your own duty", says Tuka, "O people, I'm telling you a principle."

Buddha says, anger and attachment lead to hatred and suffering, as anger leads to hatred and hatred leads to suffering and anxiety.

Chapter 10: Love and Marriage

I find the best way to build a relationship is through a common background. I see two people coming from the same background with the same moral values as going a lot further than a couple that has little in common. This is usually the foundation of a relationship and it keeps one another interested. The two keep mutating and exchanging their ideas, thoughts, feelings, and actions and start creating harmony. A new rhythm, a new music starts playing. They keep adding and subtracting various qualities within themselves through creativity, communication, and the wisdom that comes through doing things and especially when doing things together.

 The idea of a sustainable marriage is one with love, faith, respect, intimacy, friendship, playfulness and commitment. It is about making the grass greener on one's turf, taking more self-responsibility for one's happiness without blaming and keeping the continuity and growth in a relationship. This needs a matured frame of mind, with a wider worldview, combining pragmatism with creativity, mechanical with electrical engineering, simplicity and integrity with dynamism and courage, strength and confidence to keep growing and flowing.

It is necessary to understand one's needs and not try to fulfill the lack of it through acquiring external objects or people, but rather through developing those within oneself or between each other. This helps in developing individuality, focus, originality, and mental strength rather than wasting time, money, and energy in keeping up with the Jones's syndrome. It allows one to be more giving, matured, experimental, a calculated risk-taker, responsible and yet childlike-acting through this drama of life beautifully and yet seriously. It makes one self-organized, self-regulated, naturally young and mentally strong forever.

Even as far as children are concerned, they need to be guided and protected along the five principles of developing, protecting, and correcting the body, mind, emotions, intellect, creativity, and consciousness so that they find purpose and motivation in leading a spirited life in full freedom. Protections are also taken to be safe and not lose one's way in the "dreary desert sand of dead habits" which could parch souls and cause one to fall victim to sex, drugs, violence, or rebelling without a cause.

Keeping those guidelines in mind early in life, they would learn to reflect, introspect and contemplate and make effective use of their time, education, resources, plans, privacy and freedom. They would be able to learn to regulate their thoughts, feelings and actions and find meaning and purpose of money, innovation, technology, sports, education, design, creativity, policies and regulations and in order to be able to debate positively and suggest changes instead of falling for peer pressure or blind consumerism and proving one's self-worth through external means.

This would lead to the development of the right balance of freedom with human values without unnecessary rebellion and would also help parents not to force their expectations. Rather, a positive exchange of ideas and mental or energy blocks can make the family a positive playground of learning and innovation, making the next generation take things ahead. This would allow for the development of controlled aggression and calculated risk-taking abilities with calmness, wisdom, peace of mind and with a problem-solving ability. This would suppress superficiality and mediocrity and would promote a zest for life and living all the time.

Kahlil Gibran says, "Two lovers are like two pillars in a temple. They support the same roof, but they are aloof; they are not together." He further says, "Your children are not your children. They are the sons and daughters of life's longing for itself. They come through you but not from you. And though they are with you, yet they belong not to you. You may give them your love but not your thoughts. For their souls dwell in the house of tomorrow. You may strive to be like them, but seek not to make them like you. For life does not go backward."

Chapter II: Cultivating Emotional Balance

Daniel Goleman, in his book, *Destructive Emotions*, starts with a question to the Dalai Lama. He asks, "How do you define mental health? Mental health per se has not been studied in psychiatry. Instead, the focus of research has been on mental disorders, and mental health has largely been defined as absence of psychiatric illness. The tools offered by psychiatry are intended to attack the symptoms of emotional suffering and not to promote emotional flourishing". In my opinion, this is a corrective approach to mental and emotional health.

The Dalai Lama says in the book, *Destructive Emotions*, "The Buddhist way, by contrast, states that there are many clear criteria for mental and social well-being, as well as a set of practices for achieving it. When it comes not just to understanding mental afflictions and how to grapple with those, but also how to move into exceptional states of mental health".

In my opinion, this is more of a preventive approach to mental and emotional health. The Dalai Lama further says, "The criteria to distinguish between constructive and destructive emotions is that it is right there to be observed in the moment when a destructive emotion arises—the calmness, the tranquility, the balance of mind are immediately disrupted. Other emotions do not destroy equilibrium or the sense of well-being as soon as they arise, but, in fact, enhance it—so that they would be called constructive".

Also, there are emotions that are aroused by intelligence. Having compassion for all beings, causing them no unnecessary hurt, nor needless harm, is aroused by pondering on suffering. The Dalai Lama says in the book, *Destructive Emotions*, "When the compassion is actually experienced, it is true that the mind is somewhat disturbed, but deep down there is a sense of confidence. A consequence of such compassion, aroused by intelligent reflection, is that the mind becomes calm".

In helping those who are suffering or disadvantaged, actually, we ourselves, become awakened in the process of helping those who seek to make real their own potential. This is achieved in valuing true friendship and fulfilling our obligations, rather than in striving with egotistical motive. This is also achieved by refraining from needless competitiveness, from contriving for self-advantage, and from subjugating others.

An important aspect of Buddhist practice is to accept transience, the inevitable, and the irrevocable in knowing that change exists in everything. We should negate the barriers to our awakening, discover the positive in the negative, and seek a meaningful purpose in what we do.

Dalai Lama says in the book, *Destructive Emotions*, "There are emotions other than compassion that preserve or reinforce the calmness of the mind. Renunciation is another. It is more like a spirit of emergence. One recognizes the nature of suffering, but also senses the possibility of emerging from this ubiquitous vulnerability to suffering—this is why it is called a spirit of emergence. There is an enormous amount of emotional content in it. It is a profound sadness with respect to the mundane".

Another practice that reinforces the calmness of the mind includes seeking liberation from the negative passions of hatred, envy, greed, pleasure, pain, fame, praise, blame, rage, and especially, delusion, deceit and sensory desire.

When still, we need to be as the mountain; when in movement, we need to be as the dragon riding the wind. This is a kind of invulnerability and is not situation dependent.

We also need to be just and honorable, and we should take pride in what we do, rather than be proud of what we have accomplished. We should have humility and respect and should give thanks to those from whom we learn, or who have otherwise helped us.

Daniel Goleman writes in the book, *Destructive Emotions*, "The Buddhist system of psychology has some very precise lists of wholesome and unwholesome mental factors. Wholesome factors are constructive emotions, like faith in oneself, self-confidence, buoyancy or flexibility of the mind, an ability to feel a sense of shame, conscience, nonattachment, nonhatred, the absence of delusion and wisdom. In addition, there is a mental factor listed as nonviolence, similar to nonhatred. Then there is vigor or zeal, buoyancy, equanimity. And then we have conscientiousness—concern whether in the body, speech and mind you are falling into virtue or nonvirtue".

The Buddha's path takes up residence in these four states of consciousness celebrated as sublime abodes—loving-kindness, compassion, joy, and equanimity. Equanimity counters strong feelings of attraction or attachment that create equilibrium in the mind. The scholar Buddhaghosha points out that these are practical means by which an individual may step out of his narrow 'I' to realize the larger oneness of life.

We need to seek neither brilliance nor the void; we need to just think deeply and work hard. We should seek to be aware at all times, like the lion which only seems to sleep, and at all times we should let the mind be like running water.

Organized religions may be good for a start in people's lives to create some grounding, develop some knowledge, character, wisdom, sense of discrimination and other good qualities which Vedanta says is "swaguna bramhan" (one with good qualities). Once one reaches that level of confidence and develops faith over one's own self, one needs to go to the next stage, which is basically "nirguna bramhan" (one without any qualities). Thus, with the initial grounding, one becomes mature and confident and is capable of being free and adventurous and, yet, intelligent and responsible—qualities needed in order to navigate in the secular world. At this stage, one also drops one's own ego, as one does not feel proud of one's qualities in being dogmatic anymore. This is also called the "nirvana" or "advaita" philosophy. The real communism of existence is what prompted Jesus to say, "Be poor in spirit". It is the state of Socrates.

We need to end the political corruption of religion and allow for the most enlightened and concerned people, who want to take the challenge of humanizing themselves, to be allowed to declare their religion as just "*human*" and their citizenship as "*global*". It should not be a lifetime, organized deal. Religion should move into the realm of inner psychology and philosophy rather than just outer sectarian groups.

To reduce conflicts between individuals or families or societies or nations, I think we can have small, demilitarized zones protected by militaries of both countries ,which are the causes of conflict, rather than doing this on a mass scale. The DMZ can be used. People in all these regions will have their religion as "human" and citizen as "global", thus converting all areas of conflict into universal R&D centers. This could be applied in Kashmir/Palestine/Kosovo/Tibet. The huge amount of money, time, and energy that is spent in talking about religion, wars, nationalism, patriotism, weapons, freedom, faith, self-determination, and socialism could be invested in communication, sports, creativity, understanding, human development, art, music, language, science, health, technology, building design, literature, poetry, and research and development. Technology can transform our consciousness at the speed of light and can convert ideas into reality by being virtually present anywhere in the world.

The various insecurities and psycho-somatic illnesses in our life are caused by ego, greed, anger, and jealousy crawling in our sick minds. The only way to break free from this is to cultivate physical, mental, and emotional strength through knowledge and action. Many diseases like cancer are supposed to be related to ego and anger, anxiety and guilt with depression. Other simple diseases like nail-biting could be because of nervousness. Constipation is said to be because of our tendency not to let go. The more we reflect on these negative emotions and work to remove these blockages, the more we feel real joy and peace.

Sri Sri Ravishankar in his Sudarshan Kriya programme mentions that it is the breath that unifies humanity. The breath in many ways is the manifestation of the spirit. Harmonising the body and mind with the breath enables one to develop endurance, calmness, concentration, and dynamism. The healing breath is one of the most powerful yoga asanas called "kapala-bhati", which is a heavy panting exercise with the movement of the stomach. Such an exercise also forms the foundation of singing and running. Harmonising the breath helps in maintaining the relaxed state, inspite of being in a dynamic state, and thus makes the human body as a flute or a musical instrument, and thus we can work on developing our body, mind, emotions, intellect, creativity, and consciousness at every moment through the various situations we face or take ourselves through, and can then let others develop the same and build systems and resources for doing the same collectively without causing damages. Such a strategy could help in building positive, human relationships, work ethics, purposes, habits, destinies, responsibilities, senses of concern, as well as a sort of collaborative setting in which each is a student and each is a teacher, as well. As all conflicts start in our mind through pre-conceived notions as shown in the movie "Crash", we can try to break free of all these barriers in order to strive for this constant, life-long urge for growth and creativity through interdependency.

As Gary Zukav writes, "At each moment you choose the intentions that will shape your experiences and those things upon which you will focus your attention. If you choose unconsciously, you evolve unconsciously. If you choose consciously, you evolve consciously." Hence, we need to know what the human body, mind, spirit, life, and creativity is made up of and how it works to use it properly. Imagine taking the mystery out of the process that has been holding us back in its operation. We cannot run life on fumes. A good life, like a good voice, is "produced", not used randomly. Developing a coordinated independence with an individual awareness is the key to growth and harmony. As Emmett Fox said, "In our lives, we shall make the most of whatever talents we possess without either sighing for the impossible or fleeing from the inevitable." And Paramhansa Yogananda of the Self-Realization Fellowship said, "Breath is the cord that ties the soul to the flesh." Where your focus goes, your instrument will follow. Release is the freedom.

One has to keep learning, reflecting, acting, contemplating, and creating all the time to sharpen one's skills, communication abilities and, thus, cultivate emotional balance, which leads to higher levels of intelligence and consciousness. One has to be a warrior all of one's life. It thus comes through knowledge, power, charity, compassion, and a problem-solving attitude, which basically leads to the suppression of negativity and the growth of positive spirituality, and the seed within the person starts blooming slowly.

When we are required to act, we need to remember that right motive is essential to right action, just as right thought is essential to right words. We need not create burdens for ourselves or others to carry. We need act with necessary distinction, being both creative and receptive, and transcending subject/object dichotomy. We need to seek security in ourselves, rather than in others by keeping our focus on the unity of our mind, body and spirit allowing ourselves to be, so that our life may become a time of blossoming.

Chapter 12: The Art of Communication

To be a successful person, one must have great communication skills and one should be a great conversationalist. This goal is not very difficult to achieve; all that is required is to be geared up with the correct skills, style, and ammunition.

Here are some tips that will help you in making positive impressions with others toward enhancing your success:

The first important skill is to be confident and to have the skill of being able to gel in any environment, company or occasion. *Flexibility* and *patience* are two very important qualities in *life*.

The next important feature is to be a good listener. You will never be able to communicate and converse with someone if you don't listen to what that person says. You will get a chance to put in your views, but before that, be patient and listen to what the other person has to say. One should always be open to listening and *learning*. Learning is arduous. It takes guts to learn. Learning means one has to be humble.

Always think before you speak. Take time to put your thoughts together rather than blurt something out that you will have to repent saying.

When we communicate verbally with others, either in a conversation or in a presentation, our usual goal is to have people understand what we are trying to say. In order to accomplish this, we should remember the acronym KISS (Keep It Short and Simple). When we talk to others, we assume they will understand us. We know what we are trying to say, so obviously our message will get through. Right? Not necessarily. People bring their own attitudes, opinions, emotions and experiences to an encounter, and this often clouds their perception of our message.

When we speak, only approximately 10% of the words we use get through to others. Spoken words are unlike written words, where a person can go over a passage several times to ensure understanding. It is our responsibility to make sure our message gets across to our audience. Therefore, if we want our message to be understood, we must be careful of the words we use.

When we communicate, we need to put ourselves in our listeners' shoes. Put yourself on the other side of the table. How would the message sound if you were not fully versed in the topic? Would you understand the message, or would its meaning be lost on you?

Be aware of the world around you and keep your current events updated so as to be able to participate in intellectual conversations, and in this way you will be able to communicate with more people. Try to make your communication a little playful and yet get the serious message across.

Don't pretend that you know everything and nod your head to everything that the other person is saying. There is no harm or shame in acknowledging that you are not aware of that topic, and, in fact, you can get to learn something new. Learning means one has to be ready to drop the old; one has to be constantly ready to accept the new intelligently.

Stay away from gossiping, and also indulge in intelligent and healthy conversation.

Understand the difference between "constructive emotions" and "destructive emotions". Always bring logic and rationality in your conversations, be centered, and promote positive, creative thinking and "constructive emotions". You don't want to get caught up in arguments and fights. Always focus on "constructive emotions".

When someone starts talking about problems, be a good listener but don't jump into offering advice. If someone does ask for your advice, share a similar experience and intelligently give some advice based on your knowledge and abilities. But you should have conviction about it.

The most important thing is to be you.

Chapter 13: Fasting and Feasting

A person who believes in fasting becomes obsessed with food. Now, going beyond food is good, but fasting cannot be the way. We need to eat right to live and not live to eat.

Wrong food will create pain and discontent, and our hunger is not satisfied because hunger needs nourishment, not food. And hunger does not bother much about taste, which is basically pleasure. The basic thing is whether it suits our body, and whether it gives our body the needed energy. If pain is an iron chain, then pleasure is a golden chain.

There are people who believe in fasts—they destroy the body. And then there are people who go on eating rich foods and also destroy the body. The endless cycle of fasting and feasting continues. There are people who do both. Buddha says do not go to either extreme of indulgence or repression. Chart the middle path, which is transcendence.

Krishnamurti says in the *Little Book of Questions*, "Food is the number one enemy of man. We eat too much and we eat for pleasure. The body does not require so much food. Less food will not harm us, but more will certainly kill us faster. Harsh fact is the greatest teacher. It is that which will spur us into action. Man eats for pleasure. Our food orgies are no different from our sex orgies. Everything that we do is for pleasure, and for pleasure one has to use thought which creates problems as one cannot have pleasure without pain. It is physically impossible to make pleasure last forever."

People eat certain kinds of food or meats during certain times of the day or during certain weeks or months or years just because they belong to a certain religion or sect or caste. Their religion is based on what happens inside their kitchen, and it is a real embarrassment going out to eat with them sometimes. They do not eat based on their calorie intake or protein intake or the sodium or fat or cholesterol content in the food vis-à-vis their lifestyle, profession, or whether they are into sports or athletics and their health conditions. Many a time, I have seen that their food, which they take in the name of some god or religion, is usually loaded in salt, sugar, oil, and fat. All this is going on in the name of organized religion, which I call organized madness and insanity.

We need to remember to renew the source in order to retain good health. As the American philosopher, Henry David Thoreau said in his book, *Walden Pond*, we need to "simplify" our lives. We need not go to the forests as Thoreau did, but we probably need to bring the forest, simplicity, and living in harmony with nature in our daily lifestyle.

Thoreau writes in *What I Lived For*: "I went to the woods because I wished to live deliberately, to front only the essential facts of life, and see if I could not learn what it had to teach, and not, when I came to die, discover that I had not lived".

Chapter 14: Man is NOT a machine

Osho says, "Man functions through habits, not through awareness. He functions through his past and not through his spontaneity. Man does not look at the present moment, man is not responsive to reality. Man goes on living in old ideas, man lives through habits".

Men have fixed ideas, sometimes based on religion, sometimes on nation, sometimes on caste like untouchables, sects, job types. People have been doing the dirtiest work in carrying latrines and have been called "untouchables". Whereas nations like China and Vietnam have implemented compost toilets, which are ecological as they do not waste water like flush toilets and use the recycling power and nutrients which should be called "humanure". Recently, on my way back from Maine, I found a beautifully designed one from Clivus Multrum Inc., Lawrence, MA, USA.

In my opinion, the idea of composting, organic farming, and solar energy gets more involved and interesting when we try to see life scientifically, as in the form of microbes in biology or chemistry and physics, temperature control, ecology, environment, sustainability, aesthetics, disease control, and water conservation and start taking pride in life and knowledge. We then stop looking at it as a pit toilet for the poor who cannot afford and basically distract ourselves with virtual reality and consumerism. Only such engaged effort makes it innovative and fun. We can then develop tools, technologies, habits, lifestyles and economics around the whole system and associate a sense of pride with the same.

I also believe that religion in the 21st century should shift to the realm of human anatomy, physiology, psychology, and philosophy using creativity and communication as a means of constant development of the body and mind and should fight ego, grief, death, disease and negativity in trying to harmonize oneself with the collective, both human as well as nature.

It is really funny that people eat the same food, go to the same school, do the same work and yet try to categorize people on the basis of religion, no religion, as worshiping, liberal, conservative, and it goes on and on. Every developed country is secular. Even communist countries like Cuba and China produce world-class athletes, Olympians. With the US embargo, Cuba manages to deliver Universal Healthcare and create systems out of solar energy and has gender equality where 60% of its doctors are women.

Krishnamurti says in the *Little book of Questions*, "To be oneself requires extraordinary intelligence. One is blessed with it. No one can give it; nor take it away from us. He who lets that express itself in its own way is a "Natural Man". That beaten track will lead us nowhere. There is no oasis situated yonder; one is stuck with the mirage. The world's problems are nothing but extensions of our personal problems. All gurus, clerics, priests, preachers are welfare organizations providing petty experiences to their followers. The guru & preacher game is a profitable industry; try and make 2 million dollars a year any other way. That messy thing called "mind" has created many destructive things. By far the most destructive of them all is God. God is the figment of man's fertile imagination. When belief does not produce the results one expects of that, one introduces what is called faith. That means hope".

Can we build anything on "hope"? To have only pleasure without any pain is just not possible. That is why we have invented enlightenment, eternal happiness, and God, which is the ultimate pleasure.

Krishnamurti says in the *Little book of Questions*, "Real silence is explosive; it is not the dead state of mind that spiritual seekers think. This is volcanic in nature; it's bubbling all the time—the energy, the life—that is its quality. The line of demarcation between the madcap and mystic is very thin. One is a clinical case and the other is on its way. Having a bath is a sensual activity. The so-called religious person makes a big deal about holy dips, baptism and pilgrimages. Rather watch those soap commercials where all those guys endlessly flaunt and highlight the pleasures of a good bath. All these gurus, clerics, priests and preachers are offering us a new oasis. Soon we will find out that it is no different from other mirages; adding momentum towards destroying ourselves."

Chapter 15: Poverty of the Mind and Heart

Ramakrishna said, "Currency is the Earth and Earth is the Currency". Osho says, "To be rich is about changing focus from having to being. One can have the whole world and yet remain a beggar. This does not mean renounce the world because those who renounce their mind also remains focused on having". People control us by giving money and by not giving money. Hence, we need to use money as currency or current to explore the meaning that we are seeking out of life.

Once one drops the ego, one does not lose anything; one only loses a disease. When one drops greed, one doesn't lose anything; one only loses a disease. When one drops anger, one doesn't lose anything; one only loses a disease. Each time we drop things like this which we have, we become richer.

When greed disappears, sharing comes into existence. When anger disappears, there comes into existence compassion. When hate, jealousy, and possessiveness disappear, there comes into being love. John Lennon says in his famous song Imagine: "Imagine no possessions, I wonder if you can, No need for greed or hunger, A brotherhood of men, Imagine all the people, Sharing all the world…You may say I'm a dreamer, but I'm not the only one, I hope someday you'll join us, And the world will live as one".

One has got only oneself. And that self expresses itself in many, many dimensions—in sharing, in love, in compassion, in creativity, in learning, in knowledge, in applications—then money brings meaning.

Only a person who has developed self-control is evolved. That person has explored life in various dimensions, has developed power over one's own self, and has gotten over one's animal heritage. Such a person should think of taking up leadership or governance.

In general, we believe that power over others is more important. But in reality, what is more important is self-governance; that is, power over one's own self. Only a person who can manage one's own self can delegate and manage others.

A person who tries to seek governance or leadership position because of ego, power, or wealth will only cause self-deceit, self-destruction, and this will lead people to unreality and jingoism in the name of religion, nation, race, language, past, wealth, inheritance, and family.

Such people are the children of the past and not the visionaries of the future. To be living in the present and moving toward the future, one needs to engage in creativity, communication, learning, unlearning, growth, wisdom and not the perennial maintenance of the status-quo. One cannot afford to be dogmatic or just claim superiority because of being born in a particular family, race, or religion.

What really matters in life are one's own thoughts, feelings and actions, including what one does, how one performs, works, and how one acts and not what connections or inheritance one has. Those things are just excuses to justify lethargy.

Chapter 16: Meditation and Compassion

Meditation to me is about making—reflection, contemplation and introspection—one's second nature. It is about seeking answers to the following two questions before committing any action. They are:
Does my action harm myself?
Does my action harm anybody else?
To answer the first question, we can try to evaluate the effect of say—our work, action, lifestyle, diet, habits, consumerism, hobbies, activities—to the following components of our own human self.
They are:
(A) body, mind, emotions, intellect, creativity and consciousness. To answer the second question, we try to evaluate the same set of things against others and other things around us. They are:
(B) a fellow human-being (and every other living being and wildlife and nature and environment as rationally as possible).

To me, keeping oneself aware of the qualitative and quantitative effect on Section (A) keeps one focused on the *individual quest* for inner fulfillment, growthm and satisfaction. And Section (B) keeps us balanced with our *collective interdependent whole.*

I think such a model, with an underlying theme of *creativity and communication,* can make us a more upright and enlightened world citizenry and is a more preventive approach to our goal of growth and success and assists toward being non-violent and responsible.

We need to learn to silence our mind by developing endurance, focus and concentration. As long as we clearly understand the consequences of our thoughts, feelings, and actions and reflect on every movement of ours and its impact on our own—body, mind, emotions, intellect, creativity and consciousness—we will always be striving to do the "right" thing as we will have that intense desire to see our own development. Hence, we become responsible to ourselves and, in turn, to society as well.

This kind of deep awareness, alertness, sensitivity, creativity, purposefulness and passion leading to the development of human character and human values is, itself, meditation. As we gain experience, knowledge, wisdom and strength, we strive to break more barriers, be more confident and seek the courage to be; we defend ourselves and our convictions. We are no more driven by external stimulation, but evolve from within.

In modern times, many times we see development more as material growth and the accumulation of money and material wealth. But we fail to see materialism as a means rather than the end in itself. We fail to understand that development is about the growth of the human mind, human spirit, and human creativity and, thus, our constant urge to learn, act, grow and evolve from within. Thus, we are unable to free ourselves from the repeated cycle of violence which manifests in various forms —psychiatric and mental disorders, wars, arms, pollution, drugs, accidents, road rage, murder, rape, terrorism etc. We need to learn to deal with negative thoughts and *start responding and stop reacting.*

Hence, in my opinion, unless we achieve this basic, *"freedom of mind"*, economic and political freedom do not have much meaning. It is going back to the dark ages again in the name of freedom and democracy. Democracy, then, just becomes a matter of numbers. Blind propagating blindness. We should clearly understand that systems do not bring people up. It is the people who need to be aware of their own inner being, psychology, intelligence, character and values. And that can come only through education and work.

Otherwise, fixing the Outer without fixing the Inner is simply patch work. Some extraordinary people put all their energy into fixing the system, but it all goes to waste unless the system promotes participation and unless each individual strives for enlightenment.

In my opinion, any work that one does intelligently and with full concentration is meditation. Once we appreciate every moment of our lives and are aware and feel responsible for every thought, feeling and action which basically leads to reflection, contemplation and introspection, that—itself— is called meditation. We need more playgrounds, gymnasiums and marathons, music groups, art galleries, architects, and we need to develop communication skills, theatres, science, technology, and healthcare. The rest of all of this excessive talk of the spirituality and religion business is all humbug.

Hence, in my opinion, the following areas need to be introspected:

(1) Importance of exercise and sports and its impact on discipline and mental strength.

(2) Importance of learning to occupy one's mind with constructive activities.

(3) Importance of understanding money only as a tool to promote creativity.

(4) Importance of understanding problems as opportunities to apply our brains.

(5) Importance of cutting down the negative side of every situation, and learn and grow.

One of my strongest convictions is that in order to reduce violence in society, and in spite of so much development and comfort in our lives, we need a secular, humanistic philosophy in our education system which bears neither left nor right, but keeps a centrist path, constantly reminding to re-evaluate our priorities in life and in order to move from a theological or ritualistic form of religion toward a more secular and wisdom-oriented philosophy with a scientific basis. We need not be dogmatic or be stuck to our inherited religion. Religion in the 21st century should move into the realm of ideas and concepts, which leads to the development of the body, mind, and spirit rather than temples, churches, and mosques.

Life should not be just about getting entangled in the endless cycle of production and consumption, where economics becomes the new organized religion. GDP should also measure the number of trees destroyed, or the environmental degradation caused by consumerism when not balanced with conservation and creativity. It should also have mechanisms to measure the impact caused by the rising number of sick or prisoners in the jails. It should also have ways to measure the power of debates, the strength of marriages, the power of living life to the fullest without destruction but assimilation. The impact of technology in reducing pollution, by increasing public transport, by telecommuting, by increasing the quality of life of normal human beings with the least amount of resources.

As Tagore wrote in his song, "I have traveled many countries for many days, I have spent a lot of money in my travels, but I have just missed seeing the beauty of a dewdrop on one rice stick in the paddy field just two steps away from my home."

Basically we need to understand that c reativity and problem-solving is humanity.

Unless we reflect on the consequences for our actions, as Alicia Keys sings so beautifully in her song "Karma", then change comes through violent means. It is the freedom of mind which keeps liberty alive. Freedom of religion truly means freedom from religion.

Whenever the world has gone through decadence and irrationality, exploitation, lethargy and then revolutions have happened. A free-thinking society can be easily transformed over time to a "fascist" society when complacency and false ego sets in.

Repeatedly, the free-thinkers, whether the Buddha, or Socrates, or Jesus, or Europe's "renaissance" or the founding fathers of America, and many poets, artists and philosophers struggled for Light. As Jesus said, "What you do to the least of us, you do to me." Hence, that makes us expand our consciousness universally.

The key point to understand is nothing should turn us into mobs, slaves, or prisoners. Whether it be politics, economics or religion. May we see the sun around us all the time, and may we strive to move away from darkness and go toward light. That is the only route to "peace".

It is time we need to pursue aggressive secular humanism in order to keep the light of humanity alive, rather than politics and polarization, we need creativity and assimilation. In case we want to pursue the development of our body, mind, emotions, intellect and creativity and preserve the environment, wildlife and humanity we need to think deeply.

Where did we go right? Where did we go wrong? How do we keep our balance? How do we pursue rationality, clarity, and moderation? Freedom means to create, explore, build. Do we want to pursue change through responsibility, reflection, creativity, education, communication and non-violence, or do we we want to be back in partisan politics?

The choice is ours. We can create any world we want. The conflict is always in our mind. We need to first become a witness and seek freedom from the mind to start creating life. We need to learn to avoid repeating history, and the same mistakes, again and again. Dissent and protest are feedback mechanisms for corrective actions. It comes through music and films, as well. As Martin Luther King said, "Our lives begin to end the day we become silent about things that matter", and Thoreau said, "What is the use of a house if you haven't a tolerable planet to put it one?" We need to start nation-building right at home.

The world is one family (Vasudhaiva Kutumbam) and is home to society, nation, and world.

Chapter 17: On Pilgrimages

Why do we even encourage all these pilgrimages in the 21st century? Instead, why do we not come up with new, productive ways of building the body, mind, and spirit? Encourage marathons, long distance runs/walks, hiking, rock climbing, cycling…do things systematically applying our own intelligence that benefits the body, mind and spirits truly.

That is what religion should be about. Rather than taking all these holy dips, one can join a public swimming pool instead.

Why don't we and change our focus to creativity, sports, science, technology, art, architecture, music, poetry and literature. God or Divinity or Creativity has to be realized within an individual through maturity, understanding, work, knowledge, wisdom and creativity. It does not matter how rich you are or how poor you are, you call yourself a theist or an atheist. We still continue leading miserable lives in the name of religion. We do not even acknowledge it and live in self denial.

Sports can be meaningful only if it has a meaning in the consciousness. Otherwise, we just promote spectator sports. This has ruined the basic culture of sports and its understanding and effect on an individual—in terms of our understanding of team, strategic planning, growth, flexibility, and individuality.

Basketball is not only a sport filled with excitement, slam dunks and unbelievable athletes, it also takes training in agility, balance, strength, and speed. It involves circuit training of the upper and lower body with bursts of speed and agility drills! And so, with field hockey and soccer. The so-called religious countries are, in general, a pleasure-seeking people with no interest in sports as a part of daily life. They would like their sportsmen to win medals but have no interest or understanding of sports as part of daily life.

Some key benefits of sports as part of daily life are as follows:

1) Play more and pray less—you will not have high blood pressure and diabetes.
2) Developing endurance, concentration, physical, mental and emotional strength.
3) Decision-making abilities and conflict resolution capabilities.
4) Problem-solving and creative abilities.
5) Sportsman spirit and human consciousness.

Chapter 18: Beyond Nations and Religions—Global Citizen

When John Lennon sang the song "Imagine", all the people living in peace where there was no religion and countries, he was probably a dreamer. But today, I suppose there are more and more people in this world who believe that this dream could well become a reality, and it is worth fighting and living for. When Tagore questioned blind ultra-nationalism versus internationalism during the freedom struggle, not many people could digest it. Today, that myriad-minded man is considered by many as the icon for modern renaissance. The Buddha probably had realized this long back when he dared to question and said do not believe in anything simply because it is found written in your religious books.

Education, knowledge, wisdom, creativity, and action are the manifestations of perfection. These are all efforts that makes life grow and flow. Vivekananda said, "The world is a great gymnasium where we have come to make ourselves strong". We cannot build a system by just passing laws and legislations but by making us aware of the human character and human values. That is our intelligence, creativity and consciousness. This is the first step to get out of the clerk and mob mentality and move on to creativity, team and individuality.

What this book tries to propagate that ever-shrinking world, we need to pick the best global values and transform ourselves to global citizens or citizens of the world. Wisdom and compassion and the never-ending urge to learn and be open to ideas and giving new ideas should be the way of life. People without borders could well become a reality one day. At the same time, one should always be on guard and believe in physical, intellectual, and spiritual strength as self-preservation will always remain the need for a long time to come. In this practice of non-violence, one should never drop guard, and, hence, one should always be alert, protected, and aware of any unforeseen event.

The martial arts have always been deeply rooted in Buddhism and Taoist practice. This is evident in the warrior codes, precepts, and tenants of the various martial arts traditions. Martial arts, although translated literally to mean "the art of war", is truly an art of peace. A warrior strives to reach above himself, his false perceptions, his adversaries his highest achievement is not one of victory, but one of absolute truth.

*

A warrior, once a warrior, will always be a warrior.

A warrior is the epitome of controlled compassion and controlled violence.

A warrior speaks from the pure heart and mind, transcending the ego.

A warrior is one of great discipline.

A warrior has not the luxury for excuses.

A warrior recognizes the differences between the meaningful and trivial.

A warrior can never afford fear; he lives in poverty of fear.

A warrior learns how to defend before the attack.

Chapter 19: Conclusion of the Journey

The journey is an interesting one as we reach this stage of complete fulfillment in life, and the journey must be made. It is worth every moment. One must develop one's oral as well as written communication skills so that one can express one's experiences, develop one's intuition, one's philosophy both in professional as well as personal life. The world will soon be filled with the diaries of these travelers reaching out to each other in various ways and forms.

When millions understand the truth that ego, grief, death and disease are perennial problems in life, and they have to be tackled with science, technology, education, sports, healthcare and economics so that people can focus on the development of their body, mind, emotions, skills, talent and creativity, real change will start coming in this world.

Albert Einstein said, "Any fool can make things bigger, more complex, and more violent. It takes the touch of a genius—and a lot of courage—to move in the opposite direction."

In my opinion, life is simple so long we are contented and engrossed with our human self. The moment we try to become something else, things start getting out of control.

Freedom of Mind is the goal of life. Economic and political freedom has no meaning without the Freedom of Mind. It is a waste of time arguing that communism is right or democracy is right or capitalism is right. One need not be dogmatic. Democracy works well in situations where people are well evolved, developed, have a mind of their own, are more individualistic and where there are a lot of resources at hand. Communism may be fine in a situation where a very few people have to guide and protect a lot of people, and the resources are also limited. But one can combine or transform one system to another when one feels one is prepared for it. Otherwise, democracy in a nation of blind people can only propagate blindness as it becomes a matter of numbers. At the end of the day we have to choose a system for a particular nation or situation which allows the development and preservation of the human body, mind, spirit and creativity in all.

Communism and capitalism have nothing to do with religion but with economic policies. We can have education and healthcare as communal and the industry as capital. In many ways, all of Europe, Canada and New Zealand follow this model in the name of socialism and have achieved healthcare for all. Whereas, 45 million are without healthcare in the United States. Education and healthcare are the key foundations of a stable society.

One can design a hybrid system taking in the best features of democracy, communism, dictatorship, socialism, religion, and many more. Each system meets the needs of its people depending on the time, place, resources, economics and the state of consciousness they are in. One of the finest examples of such a hybrid system, which has yielded excellent results in a very short period of time, is the Republic of Singapore. I have found Singapore to be the safest and most crime-free city among the many places in US, Europe and Asia that I have visited. Today Singapore also boasts the highest computer and technology use and penetration in the world.

We need to develop our skills of trade without end. We need to seek unity of mind, body, and spirit and understand the merits of compassion, as well as pursue knowledge of all things, regardless of nature. We also need to integrate the practice of truth within all of our day to day activities so that we can see the truth in us and others. We should know that we are not separate from all things, but strive to flow as one with all—as water taking the shape of its container. We should know that life will always have pain, sadness, joy and solitude.

Conclusion: Wherever we undermine the power of the "self" and the power of one's own human "mind" and try to promote any kind of mob-mentality either through economics, or partisan politics or religion and undermine the importance of education, healthcare, science, research, innovation, creativity and human consciousness, then we remain slaves of our own making forever and never achieve the "freedom" which is there.

Religion in the 21st century should move in the realm of human anatomy, human physiology, human psychology, and human philosophy toward the constant development of our body and mind. Alexander Tsiaras, CEO, Anatomical Travelogue gives insights in the book, *The Architecture and Design of Man and Woman*. It has some breathtaking visualization and imagery using various non-intrusive energy techniques—MRI, sound.

There will always be people within these religious countries who will exploit the status-quo using money and nepotism and keep the feudal set-up. And to sustain this, they will partner with developed countries to promote their interests for trading resources.

Hence, democracy in such situations with a majority of people not having the education, creativity, confidence, mental and physical strength becomes a tool for manipulation and promotion of mob-mentality for vested interests. Even genocide happens, as in Rwanda.

Serious innovation, creativity, sports, athletes, research, and development becomes difficult to pursue in such countries as the resources become open to manipulation as the majority prefer consumption rather than creativity. There are few intellectual businesses.

It promotes mediocrity by the thousands and these countries are not modern in the true sense of the word. They are more west-toxicated and, hence, they remain children of the past rather than flag-bearers of the future. The colonial control is indirectly maintained.

Chapter 20: The End

Religion, to me, is about the development and preservation of the body, mind, emotions, intellect, creativity, and consciousness in an individual with a sense of concern for other fellow human beings, for other living beings and for the environment around us rationally. It is about having a sense or awareness of one's own thoughts and actions. Does my "action" harm myself? Does my "action" harm anybody else? It does not matter whether God exists or not, but what definitely matters is human character and human values and developing faith over oneself. I think that sitting silently, introspecting, reflecting and contemplating is the best, scientific and most rational form of worship, developing faith in oneself, taking total self-responsibility, not blaming, not complaining, developing an attitude of gratitude and, thus, a strong body, a strong mind and a strong heart. Life has to combine rationality with emotions, and it has to balance the head and heart.

When one is silent, then it is a real dialogue with one's own self, and it starts the process of self-discovery through introspection and reflection. Excessive robotized prayers are useless. It is just simply wasting one's time and breath. Do something else—paint a picture, write a book, build a house or road, or run a mile—that would be far better.

This book is dedicated to the triumph of the human mind and spirit and creativity.

This book salutes all the adventurers, scientists, engineers, innovators, sportsmen, athletes, poets, writers, sculptors, musicians, pilots, mariners, builders, architects, doctors, nurses, surgeons, firemen who have all made humanity realize its enormous creative spirit and potential in this great "Temple of Sweat and Dust".

A path for "global" renaissance should understand these:
(1) Pluralism: spirituality of oneness
(2) Governance and non-violence
(3) Education, art, literature, communication, creativity
(4) Technology, work, inner fulfillment, and sustainable development
(5) Sports as part of day-to-day life
(6) Healthcare (preventive and corrective)
(7) Gender equality
(8) Rights, safety consciousness, responsibility, and inner psychology

There is nothing greater and more precious than freedom. But freedom should allow one to grow, dream and innovate and not commit violence or self-destruction. We need to resolve our crisis with modernity specially when we are in a situation of being uprooted of centuries hierarchical regimentation in the name of race, religion, caste, profession. We need to be making our own path, using our own intelligence. That trodden track will not lead us anywhere. We should not fall a victim to misplaced and misguided priorities.

Chapter 21: A Way Ahead
Be a Polymath

First of all, we should know that if we cease to exercise our brain, we stagnate, and then we fall.

The time has come when we need people to be polymaths, a master in all branches of science, art, and philosophy. This would lead to the persistent growth and evolution of the normal intellect and to an evolved individual who is awake, aware, intuitive, creative, mature, courageous, and free. The person then develops a deeper understanding of diversity.

We need polymaths who have a multi-faceted passion for the sciences, arts, sports, philosophy, literature and languages. Only since we are not aware of this potential in us, and what nature has already provided for the progress of man, we continue to limit our intelligence with what has already happened in the past. Otherwise, the human mind has the capacity to exhibit intelligence, expand, excel and keep evolving forever.

Erick Schonfeld writes in a recent article titled, "The Culture of Participation", that the expressions of an emerging culture right here on Earth is one where every citizen is a publisher, photographer, programmer, or a product designer. It's a culture that is blurring the lines between amateur and professional, consumer and reator. Someday this may enable personalized fabrication of electronics, automobiles and furniture. Somebody has to figure out how to bring computer-aided design to asses.

The human mind can stop violence when it is highly expanded and well-integrated from many sides like passion for music, mathematics, art, sports, science, technology, film, theater, creativity, communication, self-expression, journalism, etc. Such evolved minds are our future leaders. In order to avert violence and plant real progress, progress which includes development of the higher faculties in human beings, it is absolutely necessary to have enlightened human beings as leaders. It is important to understand that everything impacts everything else. That is how democracy or governance, industrialization or economics and philosophy or inner psychology works in a harmonious trinity in an individual, in a family, in a society, and in a nation and in the entire world. Only then, we grow from a survivor mind-set to a creative mind-set in life.

Initially, the path of such evolution seems hard. But as we commit ourselves into and strive for progress by applying our minds through work, knowledge, wisdom, education, and experience, the growth starts picking up speed and then becomes natural to our psyche. The energy patterns in our body start to change as we start breaking free from the survivor mindset into the creative realm due to the confidence, maturity, understanding, and capability that grows out of such responsible calculative risk-taking. Then our individuality starts to grow and we do not fall victim to manipulations or political, economic, and social forces. That is when life starts to take real meaning and we seeking to create order out of chaos through innovation, understanding, and creativity.

Every human being should strive to achieve this state. My purpose of writing the book *A Religion called "Human"* has been to instill this sense of purpose and passion. The present day mind needs to instill awe and reverence in the minds of the younger generations and the population as a whole. It needs the ability to be deeply integrated.

With this thought I conclude. I can only say: try singing, music, writing something, painting a picture, designing a house, running a mile, designing a product, studying the cure for a disease, or go under the hood of a machine. And when we try reflecting on ideas, actions, and creativity, we will slowly deprogram ourselves and break free of all conditioning and be more conscious and intelligent and find the path to Enlightenment.

All physical conflicts first manifest psychologically in our mind due to various kinds of pre-conceived notions and a non-creative unpurposeful mind. The day we make our own evolution, our purpose in life, and seek our freedom of mind, most miseries vanish.

Art, music, architecture, literature, growth, sports, innovation, technology, problem-solving, and various other skills to strengthen each others' body, mind, spirit, and creativity are one of the finest ways to produce more light and less heat and cruelty. To me, that is what it is to be an ever-evolving, expanding, learning, and yearning human.

The real meaning of the lotus grows in the mud; it is the wisdom that grows in us through solving problems and using our body and mind. We can find meaning in using it to study the human anatomy, medicine, disaster management, engineering, communications, technology, design, collective as well as individual as well as interdisciplinary thinking, cause and effect, collective co-learning, abstract concepts and interdependencies.

When we are able to develop the deep interconnectedness among the various professions, streams of knowledge, education, learning and creativity and understand that by economic or political manipulation of certain professions we ourselves kill some vital interdependent professions and activities of our eco-system for our existence and coexistence, then we try to design things to reprioritize our interests.

But if we are just motivated by fame, wealth, false ego, and easy life we will always remain victims consciously or unconsciously and will never appreciate the deeper connection of art, music, sports, science, technology, language, literature, education, healthcare, and its impact on our body, mind, emotions, intellect, creativity, and consciousness.

Once we can expand our focus on such multi-dimensional growth, then we start finding true meaning in the quality of our work and its impact based on the time and function. Then we can develop more depth and a sense of concern. Then nothing would seem to be a burden as we crave to take greater challenges and start appreciating human beings and systems not merely as objects but as living, creative spirits and endeavors to contribute and learn from each other, to make the form and associated functionality better, and in time make economic adjustments to fulfill our own destiny. We learn to slow down, rather than be led with pointing fingers at corruption with no sense of purpose or conviction. Once the hypocrisy ends the violence seems like a waste.

Whether it is secular or religious, we seem to be missing the point about life and living. Life is about bringing a synergy of three things: (1) The problem or mystery that we are trying to solve or understand; (2) The state of knowledge, science, technology, research and development available to address the same; and (3) Planning and allocating time, money, energy, and resources to achieve the same at various levels with management, fallback sms, regulations and evolving guidelines with feedback systems like media or investigative journalism or audits to achieve the same and keep the continuity.

Instead using either method—whether it is secular or religious—we have been engaged in endless revolutions and violence and yet we do not learn that the ultimate goal is about learning and innovating various tools and techniques to channelize our energies creatively and productively. Maintaining status-quo or mixing or separating politics with religion does not allow for progress. It only makes us repeat history again and again. The key factor is to be able to decide whether any action or knowledge—whether it is secular or religious—does it bring forth any gain in our life or the life of other people, nature, environment and living beings? And we should be ready to discard such irrationalities.

What we need, it seems, is not just secularism but aggressive secularism, humanism, and universalism in our education system so that we get rid of the politics of religion, the religion of numbers, the manipulation of minds and the cause of irrationality and inflexibility. Let us debate on all religions and discuss democratically on things that really benefit the—body, mind, emotions, intellect, creativity, consciousness—of every human being and filter out the things which are meaningless and cause a waste of time, energy, resources, harm, death, and destruction. We will find that things are very simple and we need not make museums part of our daily life and that is when we become creative. It is high time that the intelligent become aggressive and the aggressive became intelligent so that we could bring the best values of the left and right together. The key phrase to keep in mind is to "To Think Before We Act", rather than act before we think. And it is the alignment purpose, passion and peace.

Chapter 22: The Song of Silence

"The Song of Silence"

The oceans are blue
Deep, deep blue.
And so is life.
Hurling with all its might
Into the deep, deep blue.
Twisting and turning,
Rising and falling.
Just meandering naturally.
When I was young,
Living in a farm
Growing up among the tres.
O, darling, come
Watch the rain & the sun.
The birds & the trees
All singing silently.

The world is mine
The whole mankind
Tied beautifully
Yet we can't find.
Life, purpose, and humanity
We believe in unrealistic things
Seek wisdom beyond our reach.
And yet we can't see life
Right there, in front of our eyes
In the vast ocean of humanity.
We live in the past.
Can't discover who we are.
Can't accept us just as humans.
We move on and on
And never listen to the song
That keep playing in our hearts.

Appendix: Summary of Religion

1) Religion should limit itself to human character and human values.
2) Religion is the development of the body, mind, emotions, intellect, creativity, and consciousness in a human-being with a sense of concern for a fellow human-being (and to every other living being and the environment as rationally as possible).
3) A truly religious person uses his brain to reflect, contemplate and meditate on problems and uses his/her creativity, consciousness, education, science, technology, sports, music, language, and research to come to solutions to the day-to-day problems in order to pursue growth.
4) To a religious person, life is a series of experiences of good and bad, dark and light, and one knows very well that the world will always have problems of ego, grief, disease, and death. One handles total freedom

with total responsibility and does not make excuses nor blame god.

5) A truly religious person tries to develop complete faith on his/her own self though physical, mental, and emotional strength and treats the world as a great gymnasium, where we have come to make ourselves strong. S/he addresses the poverty of mind and heart.

6) Religion is about the development of the human mind, human body, human spirit, human creativity, and human consciousness.

7) One can play hockey with full concentration, and that is meditation.

8) All the established religions are 80-100% irrelevant in the modern context.

9) A truly religious person believes that god is nothing but the universal intelligence, and he/she is part of the large eco-system.

10) There is no magic in holy books; they should be treated as any other regular books which may have some perennial wisdom.

11) Religion is for the action-oriented thinker who is eager to question, seek, and develop wisdom through one's own experience, education, work, knowledge, and creativity and he must be ready to share the wisdom with others.

12) Only a deep thinking, humanistic, and creative person is religious.

13) Economic and political freedom have no meaning without the freedom of mind.

Reference: The Energy of Life

This is another interpretation of the book regarding human religion with the chakras.

The development and integration of the various chakras (or energy centres) through knowledge, work, education, action, creativity, reflection, and introspection brings about a balance that enhances productivity and are as follows:

Chakra 1: Muladhara

The root chakra is located at the base of the spine. This chakra deals with the human potential, primitive energy, basic survival needs and our foundation. This basically involves nutrition, balanced diet, sports, exercise, regulated lifestyle for the *body's* growth. Ignoring this may lead to a significant lack of energy and can make you weak and self-destructive.

The symbolic colour: Red.

Chakra 2: Svadhisthana

The second chakra is located just slightly below the navel or belly button. This chakra is the centre of our sexual drive and emotions. This basically involves understanding the importance of emotional strength combined with physical strength as a foundation for growth. It also involves understanding destructive emotions, self-control, concern and responsibility. A deficiency of energy here may cause you to be immobilised by fear, burdened by guilt, or may cause you to be distrustful.
The symbolic colour: Orange.

Chakra 3: Manipura

The third chakra is located at the solar plexus and relates to will, power, and social identification. This basically involves self-worth, positive self-concept, corrective action to avoid repetitive mistakes, sense of purpose and direction, developing social skills, and system, ego vs eco. A lack of energy here may result in depression and confusion.
The symbolic colour: Yellow.

Chakra 4: Anahata

The fourth chakra is located over the heart and relates to love, balance, compassion, and self-expression. This is also associated with developing a "deep sense of concern" about other living beings, nature, wildlife, a voice of positive dissent for truth, justice, free-spirit, and moderation. It might help to bring rationality with good values, rather than plain raw emotions to make decisions to sustain the spirit. Little energy in this chakra may cause paranoia and indecision.

The symbolic colour: Green, sometimes pink.

Chakra 5: Vishuddha

The fifth chakra is located at the throat and relates to communication, creativity, and self-identification. This involves the release of one's breath, the real freedom to create and communicate—orally, as well as through written skills, understand the interdependency of systems and in order to seek to innovate, motivate, create, communicate, and accommodate. A blocked chakra here can cause a person to be devious and manipulative.

The colour here is blue.

Chakra 6: Ajna

The sixth chakra is located between the eyebrows at the third eye position relating to mind, intuition and heightened self-awareness. This involves development of the mind and intellect through work and knowledge and seeks constant expansion to integrate—skills, knowledge, domain and roles which help in developing an integrated personality and vision. Insufficient amounts of energy here can cause you to be oversensitive and afraid of success.

The symbolic colour: Violet.

Chakra 7: Sahasrara

The seventh, or crown chakra, is located at the top of the head, and deals with the experience of self-realisation, wisdom, understanding, and consciousness. This makes one ripe by developing all the chakras and one becomes wise and non-polarised. One does not seek meaning in partisan politics or fame in realizing one's talents or qualities. It is a state called the "nirguna bramhan". A deficiency of energy here may cause a person to become catatonic. The last four charkas are involved in the development of our higher faculties from the heart to the throat to the head. The first three are more about strengthening the lower faculties and promoting self-preservation.

The symbolic colour: White, which signifies enlightenment, and is the culmination of all the other charkas.

Afterword

A Religion Called "Human": A Case for "Positive" Secularism is a very realistic, awe-inspiring, down-to-earth, practical book written by Chanakya Ganguly based on his real life reflections and experiences—both personally, as well as professionally, religiously, as well as scientifically, through real life experience and world-wide travel, as well as through intense study, reflection, contemplation, introspection and intense creativity.

If I have a choice, then I do not belong to any nation or religion. I believe that the world and religion are One, comprised of rational, free-thinking, humanistic people with common sense. As Thomas Paine wrote, "I love the man who can grow brave by reflection, whose heart is firm, and whose conscience approves his conduct, and hence will pursue his principles unto death." At the end of the day, what really matters is: "What did I learn? What did I unlearn? How did I grow? What did I create? What did I build, teach and share to make this life beautiful?" In our quest for life, liberty and the pursuit of happiness, we can reflect on the words of Jefferson: "It is neither wealth

The message is clear: creativity and communication is humanity and is about dropping dogma, fixed ideas, and pre-conceived notions through life-long learning, intense interplay of thoughts, ideas, individualistic, as well as collective actions, democratically, with a sheer constructive motive, a willingness to learn, unlearn, teach, and grow. Other factors include a multi-dimensional flowering of the mind, spirit and creativity, as well as a fighting ego, grief, disease, death, negativity through innovation, responsibility and sense of concern.

As the Brazilian educator, Paolo Freire said, "Education is not the key to transformation, but transformation is in itself educational. We need a school that is happy, rigorous and works democratically. It is about being 'Human'."

Order the book from PublishAmerica,
www.PublishAmerica.com
ISBN # (soft cover): 1-4137-8489-5.

The author plans a sequel to *A Religion Called "Human."* It is titled: *A Path for an Engineer*, and focuses on technology, innovation, creativity, sustainable development, arts, human-computer-interaction, computer systems design, empowering the disabled, visualizing the interdisciplinary domains, high-speed information storage, retrieval and transmission, safety management, disaster recovery, simulation and modeling, compliance, regulations, corrective actions, purpose-driven education, engineering, design, planning, architecture, governance, and economy.

Sequel: *A Path of an Engineer*

In living life, we need a management principle to coexist, including an analysis of how we grow as individuals within the collective of humanity, with respect to the resources of the planet. Hence, I have focused on creativity and communication. Another thing is the concept of nation or religion, which are all virtual ideas. Majority, minority are all politics. The other issue is universally that we will always have the problems of: ego, grief, death, disease, and other negativities like anger or greed and so on and so forth. But we need to learn to develop self-control and stop reacting and start responding through reflection and contemplation, which we can call meditation, so that it eventually become habit or second nature to us. Then, we need to pursue scientific innovations, discoveries, behave responsibly and show a sense of concern in order to then solve other problems by pursuing safety consciousness and economics rather than arms and ammunitions. At the end, we want to develop our body, mind, emotions, intellect, creativity, and consciousness and use resources, education, occupation, food, music, dance, sports, exercise for the same, and at the same time, we need to remember that we are able to perform certain tasks because we have an audience for the same, and hence, we are part of the collective. Hence, we need to show a sense of concern for a fellow human-being and every other living being, the environment, ecology and wild-life around us as rationally as possible and without making a mess of this whole place. We also need to empower people more and more so that each of us starts enjoying our freedom and aloneness; we can then start to get deeply engrossed in exploring the human self. Otherwise, it is only cheating one's own self.

This is basically making religion democratic and human and is taking control of religion in one's own hands and not letting anything else control one's destiny. One can always refer to any of them for suggestions and accept the parts that make sense at that point of time. This can be from any religious or secular source. We can reject the rest when it does not make sense. This is about not being dogmatic and having fixed ideas and forming dead habits. This is freedom of the mind, or common sense. It is about being human. The other point I wanted to clarify is that

At this point here is a poem by Rabindranath Tagore: Where the mind is without fear, And the head is held high, Where knowledge is Free, Where the world has not been broken up into fragments by narrow domestic walls, Where words come out from the depth of truth, Where tireless striving stretches its arm towards perfection, Where the clear stream of reason has not lost its way into the dreary desert sand of dead habit, Where the mind is lead forward by thee, Into ever-widening thought and action, Into that heaven of freedom, my Father, let my country awake. [The last line could be reinterpreted as, Let Humanity Awake, as the poet was referring to the Indian subcontinent, but it is universal].

There are two ways to live life: One, as a survivor and the other as a creator. The survivor is always insecure and sees the world as chaotic, and the creator tends to be calm, centered, and assured, seeingthe world as ordered and taking life on a stride, looking for challenges, opportunities, problems and growth. Money and knowledge are important to create one's foundation, but eventually the drive and acceleration has to set in so that one can start finding see-throughs and breakthroughs in the path of innovation and creativity. To innovate or create from a pragmatic angle, one needs to understand and reflect upon the various self-regulating, non-regulating and human-regulating systems that drive life, technology, human beings, living beings, the natural resources, and the environment individually, as well as collectively. One also needs to understand how science, technology, art, literature, language, communication, economics, ethics, laws, legislations, engineering, and healthcare all interplay between each other to create meaning out of economics, production, consumption, occupation, discovery, and inner fulfillment. Through all of these reflections, contemplations and introspections, we can start understanding what real education, humanization, and democracy is all about. We can start understanding the democracy within our own selves, in terms of how we prioritize our thoughts, feelings and actions, and we can lend insight into what causes distortions in the same and curb our enlightened, rational, free, and humanistic thinking. The world religion comes from the Latin stem, "religio", meaning connecting to one's own self. At the end of it all we are only answerable to our own selves. Labeling democracy without deep learning and understanding stops growth, starts decadence, and breeds violence. Hence, the system has to be constantly questioned in order to get feedback on the violations, degradations, and methods that need to be adopted for corrective actions, whether in the form of education, sports, arts, or creativity.

The key point to understand is that the system should promote self-organization and self-management rather than use profiling and statistical techniques. It should not eliminate the human component of intelligence, innovation, debate, discussion, and creativity. We might then totally surrender to the system and remain complacent to all that has been achieved. Then, autocracy, negativity, and finger-pointing could potentially set in, self-responsibility could get diverted into politics and the blaming game, and the Us versus Them theory could start taking shape. People might then start romanticizing about some utopia or some golden historical past or character or incident to which they have no real connection whatsoever. Virtual and false ego could then set in due to inaction, and the hysterical clerk and mob mentality could take root. Hence, one has to be in alertness and awareness in order to hold it together.

Epilogue

I am not against money. I am totally for money. The only thing I am against is "mental blockage", where one chooses or is not able to choose a certain profession because of money and then looks down upon other people because of money with no deeper understanding of human intelligence and creativity. The beauty of the human being is the ability to create, flourish and support the same with one's heartfelt passion and deep appreciation.

This is where I start my "sequel", keeping the previous book: *A Religion Called "Human"* as a foundation. This new book tries to discover an enchanting path for the life of an engineer. Today, whatever religion or faith or profession or economic or political condition we belong to, we live in a modern house, use the light and electricity, buy similar clothes, travel in cars and buses over bridges, railroads, and highways, buy gasoline and groceries, do business between each other, and we go to school. It seems to me, that at a certain point in life, we suddenly start taking all of this for granted—as if it is all normal, perennial, and therefore nothing has to be done.

This tendency of ours to seek permanence and maintain the status-quo leads to decadence and violence. When we start living a life of deeper understanding and start appreciating every moment and all of these things we use around us, including how they improve our lives, and if we reflect on our responsibilities in not abusing the same, but rather on how to make it better and better, either by changing human habits or by making better gadgets, we start finding that path: A PATH OF AN ENGINEER.

Engineering happens in all walks of life: social, psychological, political, economical, civil, mechanical, electrical, medical, electronic, within computer systems, and in telecommunications. And there is a subtle interplay between all of these various streams of engineering. The more that we grow and expand in life, the more we break free from our narrow ideas toward a deeper understanding of this interplay in building better and better systems. The same is also true for secularism, democracy, and governance.

What calculators were used for decades ago, computers are now used for the same in these modern times. The beauty of computers and communications is that they act as a "glue" in disseminating information, analyzing facts, doing computations, and, thus, promotes inter-disciplinary roles.

Nothing should enslave us or hold us captive whether it is god or no god, money or renunciation, power or knowledge, experience or inexperience, aggression or passivity, profession or status, but each should be used positively as a tool for the liberation of the body, mind, spirit, and creativity. And that to me is true *"freedom"*. Life should be taken more as a marathon of endurance, reflection, stamina, growth, and tranquility rather than as a chaotic dash and stampede, as the world will go on forever.

> You are what your deep, driving desire is,
> As your desire is, so is your will,
> As your will is, so is your deed,
> As your deed is, so is your destiny.
> —Brihadarnyaka Upanishad IV.4.5

In the book "Culture and Prosperity", British economist, John Kay, writes that the two essential traits of wealthy nations are disciplined pluralism, the meaning of competition and cooperation that occur in a market economy and the possession of deeply embedded social, economic and political institutions.

Hence, profit making has to be balanced with humanism through the form of established institutions like banks and government social agencies, compliance, regulations, restrictions, and taxation. Thus, development should not mean, "man lives by bread alone". It should be seen more as an evolution from inside through art, science, technology, research, economics, music, acting, language, and sports.

On June 20th, 2005, Nobel laureate, Jack Kilby, whose 1958 invention of the integrated circuit ushered in the modern electronics age and made possible the microprocessor, died at age 81 at his Dallas home. His 2000 Nobel citation said Kilby, "laid the foundation of modern information technology." TI chairman, Tom Engibous, while remembering Kilby said that people whose works have truly transformed the world and the way we live in it are Henry Ford, Thomas Edison, and the Wright Brothers.

Technology with a bit of ethical imagination is possibly the greatest thing that has happened to the growth, development, integration, and evolution of mankind. Today the word processor I am using to write this document allows me to change, edit, modify, save, and reformat all at ease without the painstaking efforts of writing and rewriting and saving it on ink and paper. Every gadget from the automobile to the television, from the phone to the oven, technology is at work. Yet we seem to take things for granted.

On June 21st, 2005, a retired public school teacher who was so frugal that he bought expired meat and secondhand clothing left $2.1 million for his alma mater, Prairie View A&M, the school's largest gift from a single donor. Whitlowe R. Freen, 88, died in 2002 and retired in 1983 from the Houston Independent School District where he was making $28,000 per year as an economics teacher. Green's frugality was matched by his belief in education and dedication to young people.

It is time that we have zest in life and accept life as God and not let it wither away. We need to break free of our "feudal mindset" and learn, adapt, and assimilate with multiplicity and keep our focus on the standards of excellence, ethics, compliance, human issues, social responsibility, moderation, balance, innovation, motivation, expansion, and creativity. We should be ready to accept our mistakes and change where need be and not get stuck with fixed ideas and yet still hold ground on one's worth, striving for and pursuing them aggressively. That makes us more matured, centered, and rooted in our own being. As Socrates said, "Know Thy Self". To add to it I would say, discover ways to channelize each others' energies in this world, keeping in mind it's effect on our body, mind, emotions, intellect, creativity, and consciousness and without leaving a mess around us.

This approach will also help us in decision making, intelligent selection, and use of resources, developing our mental faculties and celebrating life and humanity in all it's diversity. It will also help us to be self-motivated, life-long learners; there would be no time left for sitting, brooding, violence, and anxiety.

At the same time, we need to create space to propagate this idea such that this playground remains available to us, as there will still be a lot of enemies to this idea of progress and that is what freedom and democracy is about, which we need to defend so that we do not slip into the Dark Ages. Such forces usually come in the form of politics and religion, combined with economic manipulation. On a positive side, politics should be involved with policy design and hence should involve highly educated and evolved professionals; religion should involve psychologists, artists, poets, writers, doctors, and athletes. Economics is a source of energy to rationalize our priorities. In life, we need a bit of all these skills, and we need to focus on our best ones.

Change and balance is always happening in this world. When we become unconscious, inflexible, and want to maintain status-quo, then change very often comes through violence and that is when reality strikes. In order to avoid violence, we need to have our consciousness clear and be open to feedback, change, needs, and we should question the root cause of conflict. The key thing to understand is that life is about the conscious liberation of the human mind, spirit, and creativity, and we need to figure out our ways.

When we analyze violence, we probably need to analyze what is our philosophy of life with regard to real issues of existence and coexistence, as well as how it reflects positively on our political and religious ideologies rather than allowing us to fall victim to a tool which could be easily used for manipulation. Our purpose in life should be clear and should show us a path that leads us to constant growth, learning, creation, wisdom, and evolution. Only a clear purpose would bring peace. Real secularism is creativity and consciousness. Communication and understanding are key factors.

BIBLIOGRAPHY

1. *Tantric Transformation: Discourses on The Royal Song of Saraha.* Ed. Ma Prem Asha, Ma Nirgun. Osho International Foundation, Rebel Publishing House Pvt. Ltd., India, 1994.

2. *The Little Book of Osho.* Ed. Ma Deva Sarito Osho International Foundation, Penguin Books India Ltd., India, 2000.

3. Dalai Lama. *Destructive Emotions.* Narr.Daniel Goleman. Bantam Books/Random House, 2003.

4. U.G. Krishnamurti. *The Little Book of Questions.* Ed. Mahesh Bhatt. Penguin Books Ltd., India, 2000

5. http://www.osho.com

6. http://www.mindandlife.org/ (MIND & LIFE Institute)

6. Communication with legislators
   http://www.iowalum.com/advocate/legislator.html

7. Chakra References
   htttp://www.balanced-energy.com/
   a_bit_about_chakras.htm

Printed in the United States
35760LVS00002B/127-216